Simon Rogerson

Project Skills Handbook

Chartwell-Bratt   Studentlitteratur

British Library Cataloguing in Publication Data
Rogerson, Simon, *1951-*
    Project skills handbook.
    1. Higher education institutions. Students. Study
    techniques
    I. Title
    378'.17'02812

ISBN 0-86238-146-0

© Simon Rogerson and Chartwell-Bratt Ltd, 1989

Chartwell-Bratt (Publishing and Training) Ltd
ISBN 0-86238-146-0

Printed in Sweden,
Studentlitteratur, Lund
ISBN 91-44-30481-1

1 2 3 4 5 6 7 8 9 10 | 1993 92 91 90 89

*Dedicated to
our daughter Jemma
with love*

TABLE OF CONTENTS

Chapter 5 "Unaccustomed as I am..."   91

Chapter 6 "It was working this morning!"   103

SUMMARY   109

Chapter 7 "House of cards"   111

Appendices   113

List of figures

PREFACE

Many courses include a project in the syllabus. The aim of the project is to provide an opportunity to develop and utilise the skills acquired from the rest of the course. In many cases, the project concerns a real practical problem which is subject to typical real world constraints. The project should be a stimulating experience for the student. It should extend beyond being an element of assessment. If the project has an audience or a purpose beyond assessment, then the student's performance is likely to be improved.

The project is probably the longest and hardest task that the student has to undertake. The onus is on the student to define the problem boundaries, to investigate possible solutions, to develop a chosen solution and to manage the project. The independence in this learning experience will only prove beneficial if the student is provided with guidelines for undertaking the project. Project Skills Handbook aims to provide these guidelines.

All projects comprise three interrelated components; technology, communication and management. Whilst technology is comprehensively covered on courses, the other two components often receive minimal attention. This situation will affect the student who will fail to recognise the importance of project communication and management. The student will exhibit warning symptoms such as: making excuses for unfinished work, frequently changing direction, filling time with other activities, blaming others for shortcomings, postponing progress meetings, deferring documentation tasks. These warning symptoms indicate the student is in trouble and in danger of not completing the project.

This book considers the major issues within project communication and management. The text is short and much reliance is placed on diagrams and checklists to aid clarity. It is hoped that the reader will find the book enjoyable and informative. The success of the book will be measured by the number of readers who do not fail their project through poor management or ineffective communication.

ACKNOWLEDGEMENTS

I would like to thank Computer Associates for allowing me to use extracts from the SuperProject Expert documentation.

During my years as a lecturer, I have supervised many student projects. Thank you to all those students. Your successes and heartbreaks have been instrumental in motivating me to write this book in an attempt to help future student generations.

To my wife, Anne, go special thanks for all your support and for your belief in me.

TRADEMARKS

SuperProject is a trademark of Computer Associates

Introduction

Chapter 1

"Why bother, I know what I'm doing?"

"WHY BOTHER, I KNOW WHAT I'M DOING?"

It is now commonplace for students to undertake extended project work as part of their study. This involves applying the skills and knowledge gained from the taught elements of their courses in an attempt to identify and provide a solution to a problem. This application must be carried out in an organised manner and the results presented in a way that gains maximum impact. Thus organisation and communication are key factors which will influence the success, or otherwise, of the project.

Effective project planning will help ensure that the project meets its objectives within the given time limits. Good planning is fundamental to the effective scheduling of a person's time. Project control is the process of monitoring actual progress against planned progress. It is the mechanism used in ensuring that the plan is still feasible by identifying deviation from the plan and highlighting the need for some corrective action.

In a project, it is people who perform the planning, controlling and assessing processes. It is also people who act as the information channels which are used to carry messages relating to these three processes. The client will explain the project problem to the student who in turn will, at some later date, inform the client of a proposed solution. The student will report progress to the supervisor who in turn will suggest new courses of action in order to improve progress. The student will describe the final results of the project to the client and the supervisor. Both will be involved in assessing the project on the basis of what they understand. Unfortunately, people are not renowned for their ability to communicate. The meaning of a communication as perceived by the sender may by very different from the meaning perceived by the recipient. Great care must be taken in communicating project information between the people involved in the project.

Half the battle is recognising the importance of good organisation and effective communication. The other half of the battle is being well organised and being able to communicate effectively. By wanting to read a book such as this you obviously recognise the importance of organisation and communication in the contexts of your own project. The object of Project Skills Handbook is to help you win the second half of the battle.

Project Skills Handbook is designed as a companion to the subject texts that you are using on your course. The aim is to give you some practical guidance in undertaking project work. There are two broad areas covered; project management and communication. To reflect this, the book is divided into two main sections. Section 1 deals with project management. You will be shown how to apply standard project management techniques to your project which is likely to be a project that only has one person, you, working on it. Section 2 deals with communication. You will learn how to deliver effective written and oral presentations of your project. Each section is subdivided into chapters, each chapter deals with a specific facet of the subject.

The book provides you with a complete framework within which you can undertake your project. You must realise that each project is different and so the project framework will have to be tailored. Use the book as a foundation on which to build your own framework.

The remaining part of this introduction is a series of visuals which should provide you with an understanding of the project framework and the associated issues that you need to address.

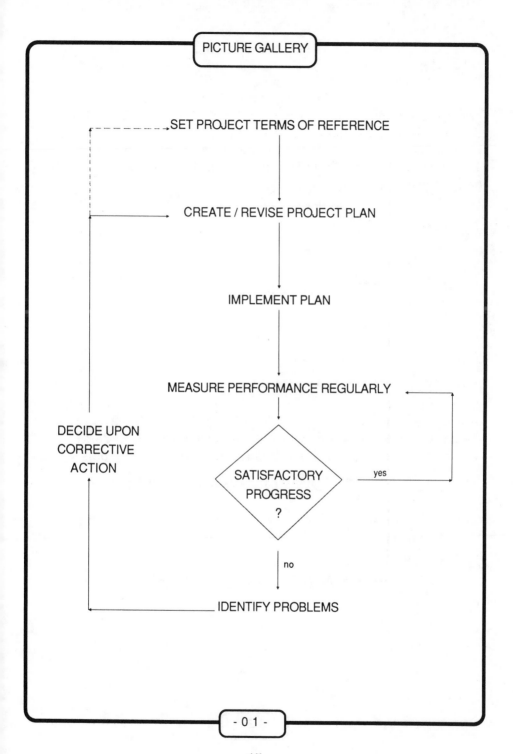

15

Planning

→ WHO will do

→ WHAT tasks

→ HOW LONG will each take

→ WHEN must they finish

16

MANAGING THE PROJECT

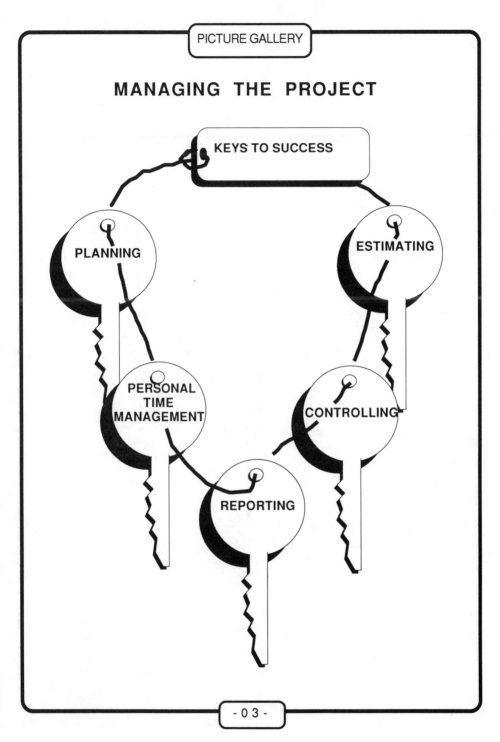

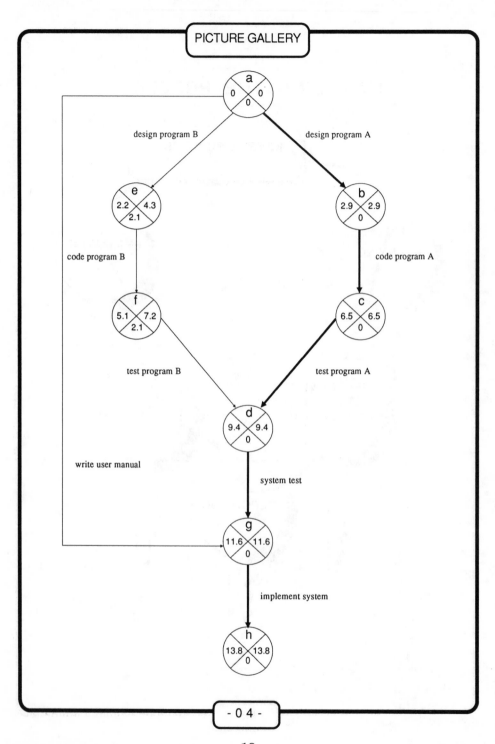

PICTURE GALLERY

PROJECT DETAILS

Summary screen

WORK BREAKDOWN STRUCTURE

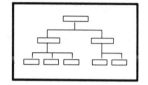

RESOURCE GANTT / HISTOGRAM

PERT CHART

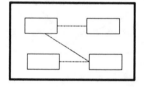

CALENDARS

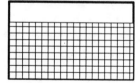

OUTLINE

Data entry screen

Project Management Software

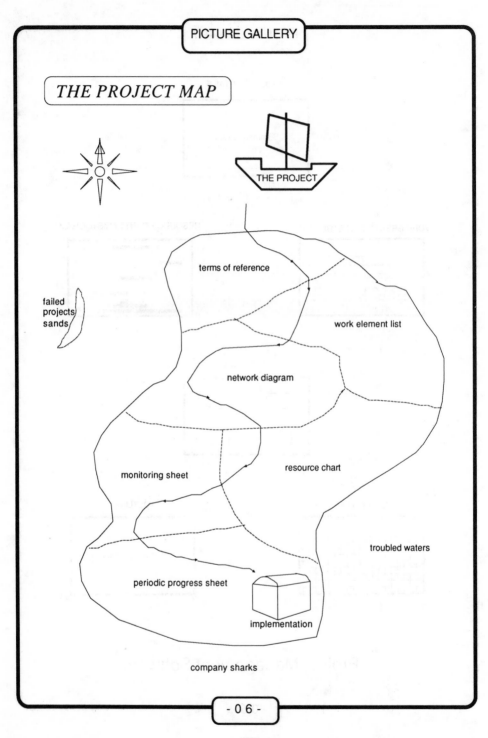

If you fail to plan

then

you are planning to fail

Time Management Model

Goals and expectations

Key areas

Work elements

Personal action plan

Diary   Time booked

Time available

What to do now

Time obstacles

lack of motivation

poor powers of concentration

indecision

lack of self discipline

poor project meetings

involvement in too many activities

irrelevant work

rush jobs

noisy accomodation

poor study environments

VISUAL MEMORY

M o n	
T u e	
W e d	
T h u	
F r i	
S a t	
S u n	

Weekly plan

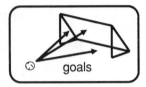

goals

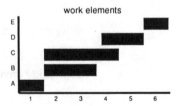

TASK of the DAY

DON'T FORGET

annual plan

work elements

Time management is about balancing

efficiency and effectiveness

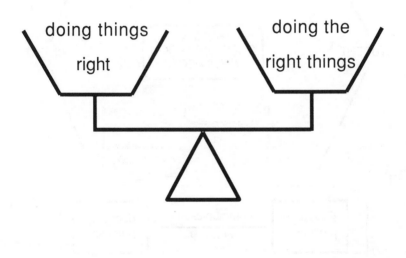

doing things
right

doing the
right things

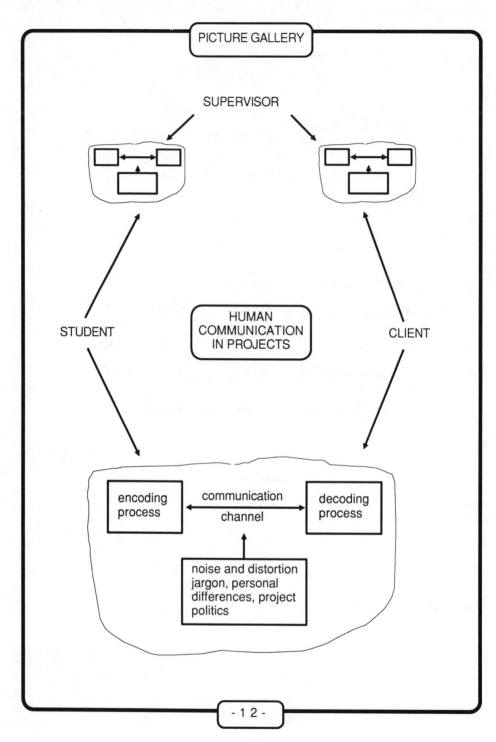

PICTURE GALLERY

SUPERVISOR

STUDENT

HUMAN
COMMUNICATION
IN PROJECTS

CLIENT

encoding
process

communication
channel

decoding
process

noise and distortion
jargon, personal
differences, project
politics

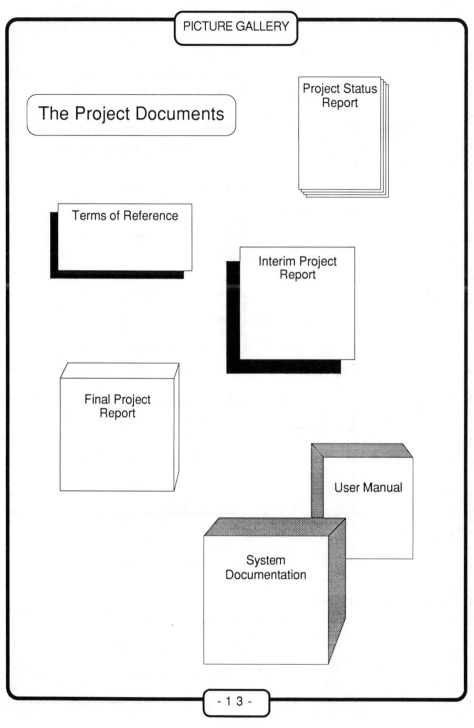

The Project Documents

Project Status Report

Terms of Reference

Interim Project Report

Final Project Report

User Manual

System Documentation

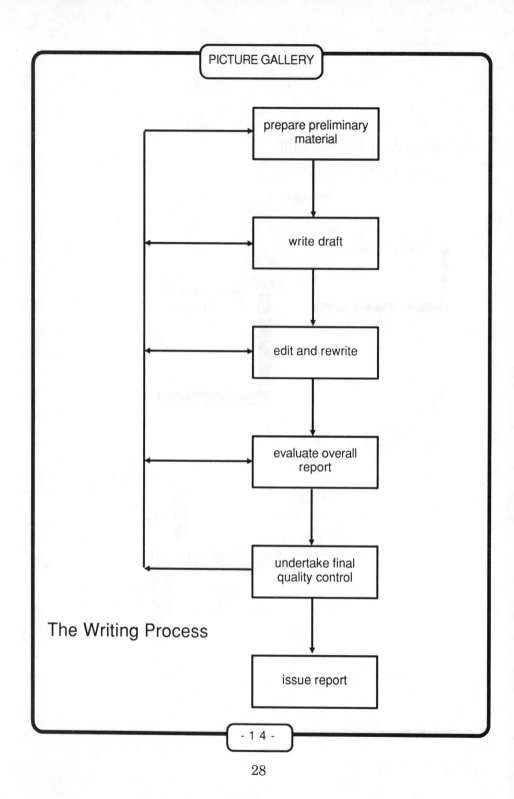

The Writing Process

QUANTITY

blue corner

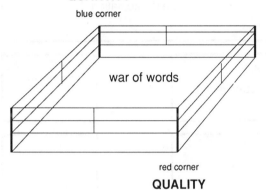

war of words

red corner

QUALITY

projects are assessed

and not weighed

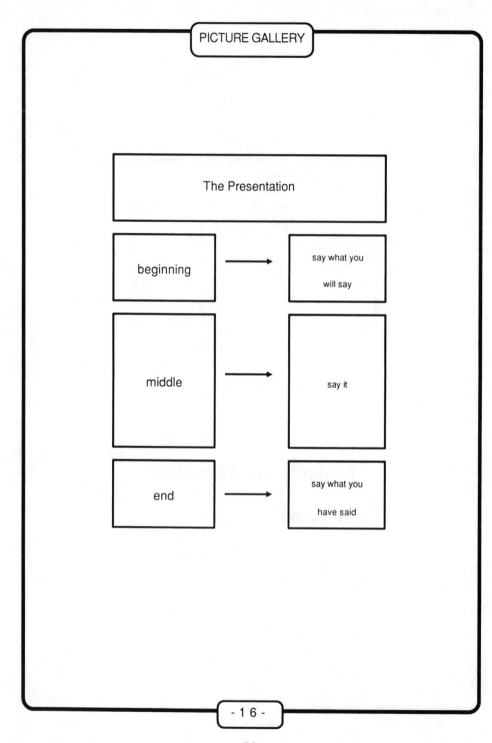

A good visual

BIG and BOLD

Clear and Concise

Stimulates Interest

Attracts attention

gets the message across

Distractions

poor visual aids

talking to the visual aid

mumbling

timekeeping

noise and interference

sidetracking

careless adlibs

non stop jokes

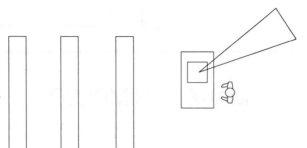

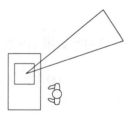

Room layouts

MAKE IT SIMPLER

complexity is the enemy of comprehension

You will never get a second chance to

create a good first impression

SOFTWARE DEMONSTRATIONS

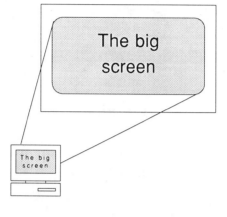

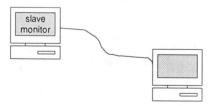

Can everyone see?

Demonstration disasters

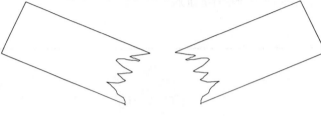

no printer

disk failure

printer failure

power failure

software error

computer malfunction

Always demonstrate to the strength

of the product

Never knock your product

someone else will try to do that

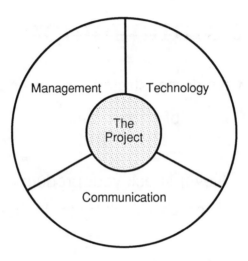

Remember to address the three elements

of the project

SECTION 1

Project Management

Chapter 2

"Where do I start?"

This chapter deals with planning and subsequent control. Standard techniques are adapted for use in student projects. Sample forms are provided which support the planning and control cycle.

Chapter 3

"If only I had time to plan."

Personal time management is crucial for students. The chapter describes a method for time management and considers the key activity areas that a student should concentrate on.

The master versions of the forms used in this section can be found in Appendix B. These forms can be reproduced as long as copyright is acknowledged.

CHAPTER 2

"WHERE DO I START?"
– Project planning and control

You have to complete your project successfully if you are to achieve success in the course that you are following. Whilst it may be true that you can seek advice and help from your tutors and fellow students, the onus is very much on you to perform effectively because you are the major resource of the project. You are now on your own, so where are you going to start?

Your answer to this question may well make or break the project. It may be very tempting to dive straight in and start thrashing around from one task to another but this is a sure way to drown. Before embarking on any tasks you must take stock of the situation. The key to completing the project successfully is to have an effective plan which will identify what needs to be done and when it needs to be done in order that you can meet the objectives of the project. Your plan can then be used to monitor actual performance which will highlight any deviations from the plan and so focus your attention on the critical areas where corrective action needs to be taken. You must always remember that planning is not a static activity but a dynamic one. The plan will, and must, change to reflect the current status of your project. Planning and control form a dynamic cycle which enables you to assess the impact of a problem on overall progress. This cycle is described in figure 2.1.

The problem which has caused progress to differ from that planned may be so serious that you will have to change the terms of reference for the project in order for you to achieve a worthwhile result. The dashed line in figure 2.1 accounts for this. Changing your terms of reference is likely to occur infrequently.

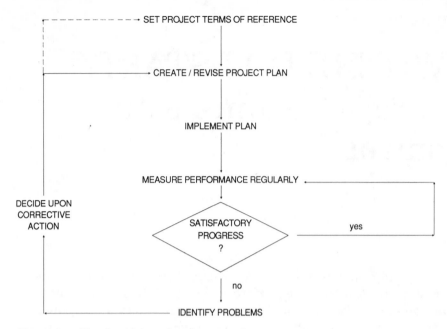

Figure 2.1 The dynamic cycle of project planning and control

Planning

You can undertake good effective planning by performing a series of activities. This series is the same regardless of the size or the nature of the project. It is the level of detail and content of activities that change with projects. Figure 2.2 summarises the series.

Terms of Reference

First you need to define and agree terms of reference for the project. Agreement will be between yourself, your project supervisor and your client (if you have one). These terms of reference will provide you with a sense of direction. Make sure that they include aims and objectives that are achievable in terms of time availability and your experience.

They should include the following information:

- Define and Agree Terms of Reference
  - aims and objectives
  - time and resource constraints
  - contacts
- Specify Phases, Tasks and Activities
  - interdependencies
  - estimates of time to complete work
- Produce Project Plan
  - critical work elements
  - check points
  - all party agreement

Figure 2.2 Planning activity checklist

Aims and objectives
You must be very clear in your mind as to the nature of the project. The information supplied in this section needs to define the boundaries of the project; which areas are to be covered and which are not. You need to be explicit in defining what you plan to achieve during the project. Wherever possible try to quantify your objectives.

Constraints
There are likely to be many constraints relating to the project. You will have numerous calls on your time and so the time available for project work will be restricted. There will be time limits imposed on you to produce interim results as well as the final product. The format of the product may well be predefined, if only in part by your client, causing the nature of the project to be somewhat different from the ideal one that you would prefer. There may be restrictions on the development tools that you can use, both in software and hardware terms. All these constraints must be identified and fully understood before you embark on the project.

Contacts
You must be sure to whom you are to report progress and for whom you are doing the project. This may or may not be the same person or

persons. There is likely to be an initial list of people whom you can contact to discuss the project.

Spend some time in drawing up these terms of reference, it will help you to clarify what has to be done. Once they are finalised, submit a written copy to all interested parties for approval. Remember that these terms of reference are not hard and fast. You should be prepared to change them from time to time, so that they reflect the current situation.

Work Elements

Now that you have decided the nature of the project which you are going to undertake, the next task is to define it in sufficient detail to create a useful plan. Your project should be split into sections or phases. Typically you might have three phases; analysis and design, code cutting and finally report writing and product presentation. Each phase should be followed by a review of the work completed during the phase so that you can decide upon any alterations of the plan for the next phase.

It is not sufficient for you just to split the project into phases because there is not enough detail for you to maintain control of the work you are to do. Therefore you must now set about dividing each phase into a series of tasks. If your project is complex with many interdependent tasks and the duration of the project is long, say more than nine months, then it is worth considering dividing each task into a series of activities which will provide you with another level of detail.

It is important that you define all the interdependencies of tasks and activities because this will dictate which can be undertaken in parallel and which have to be undertaken serially. For example the activities of writing a program are likely to be serial work elements whilst the production of each of two programs may well be undertaken in parallel.

You now know what work has to be done but do you know how long it will take? Accurate estimating of time is very important in achieving your project objectives. Start by allocating times to each of the lowest level work elements. If you have used activities then you will probably have to use hours but if you have remained at task level, then days or half days should be sufficient. This is person time, that is the total time needed to complete a work element. Person time is

Project Calendar Day	10.00	10.00
lunch	0.75	
breaks am + pm	0.75	
time reporting etc	0.25	
interruptions	0.50	
travel	0.50	
sickness	0.10	
startup/shutdown	0.25	
Total Non Project Time		3.10
Net Project Time		6.90
Weighting Factor = 10.00 / 6.90 = 1.45		
Calendar Time = 1.45 * Person Time		

Figure 2.3 Calculation of conversion weighting factor

not the same as calendar time. Person time has to be multiplied by a weighting factor to convert it to calendar time. It is calendar time that you have to use to draw up the working plan. The weighting factor accounts for all the disruptions and time wasters that reduce the person time available in a given project calendar day. An example calculation of the weighting factor is shown in figure 2.3. You need to carry out a similar calculation. Having calculated the weighting factor, it is a simple matter to multiply the estimates for each work element by this factor. Thus all estimates are converted to calendar days which is the unit of measure that you must use in the final stage of planning; devising the project plan or schedule.

Project Plan

Now that you have identified in sufficient detail the work to be done and derived estimates for this work, you can start to develop a project plan. Remember to take interdependencies into account when you are devising this plan. Planning is a prerequisite for effective control of the project. The time you spend now in developing a workable and realistic plan will greatly benefit you during the life of the project. In order to plan your project, you should compile a work element list, draw a network diagram and complete a project resource chart.

Work element list

First you need to list all the work elements that have to be completed for the project or the part of the project that you wish to derive a plan for. The list in figure 2.4 is a task list for the later stages of development during a project. Each task is given a unique number, has a description and shows both the person day and calendar day. The weighting factor of 1.45 has been used to convert person days to project days.

If only one day per week is allocated to project work then it follows that it would take 24 weeks to complete this work. If two days were allocated to project work then it does not follow that you could complete the work in 12 weeks because you have got to take interdependencies into account. You can solve this problem by drawing a network diagram.

Network diagram

A network diagram consists of a series of connecting arrows and crossed circles. The arrows represent work elements and the crossed circles represent the start and finish event for each work element.

Task	Description	Person days	Calendar days
1	design program A	2.0	2.9
2	code program A	2.5	3.6
3	test program A	2.0	2.9
4	design program B	1.5	2.2
5	code program B	2.0	2.9
6	test program B	1.5	2.2
7	system test	1.5	2.2
8	write user manual	2.0	2.9
9	implement system	1.5	2.2
	Total	16.5	23.9

Figure 2.4 The project task list

Each event can have an earliest and latest time of occurrence. These are entered into the left and right quadrants of the crossed circles. First you must draw a network diagram showing precisely the inter-connection between work elements. The network diagram in figure 2.5 is for the task list in figure 2.4.

Next you have to calculate the earliest start times for each event. Begin at the start event ("a") and place a zero in the left quadrant. Now move to the next event ("b"). The earliest time is calculated by adding the work element duration to the earliest time for the start event of that work element. You will see that the earliest time for the finish event ("b") of task 1, design program A is 2.9 + 0 which is 2.9. You will need to carry out this calculation for all events in your net-work. Where two or more work elements converge onto the same event you must take the largest value as the earliest time for that event. For example, task 3 and task 6 converge onto event "d". The time calculated via task 3 is 2.9 + 6.5 which is 9.4, while the time cal-culated via task 6 is 2.2 + 5.1 which is 7.3, and so the earliest time for the event must be 9.4 as this is the largest value.

Now you must calculate the latest times for all the events on your network. Start at the end event and place the same value that is in the left quadrant in the right quadrant. Move backwards to the next event ("g"). The latest time for this start event is calculated by sub-tracting the work element duration from the latest time of the finish event for that work element. You will see that the latest time for the start event ("g") of task 9 is 13.8 − 2.2 which is 11.6. Where more than one work element converges on an event you must take the smallest value as the latest time for that event.

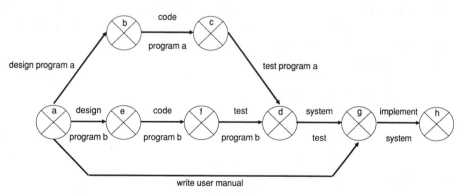

Figure 2.5 Network diagram for part of a project

47

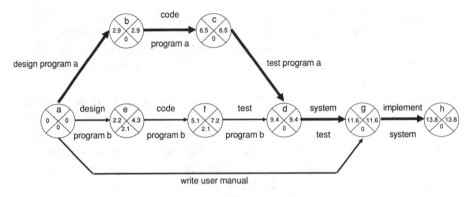

Figure 2.6 The completed network diagram

Finally, subtract the earliest time from the latest time for each event and place this in the bottom quadrant of each event. You can now identify the critical work elements in your project. These are the ones that have both start and finish events with zero difference between earliest and latest times. The work element duration must also be the same as the difference between the latest time of the finish event and the earliest time of the start event. The completed network for the worked example is shown in figure 2.6.

This completed network shows you that the project can be finished in just under 14 days assuming unlimited resources and that the tasks to concentrate on are the designing ("1"), coding ("2") and testing ("3") of program A, the system test ("7") and the implementation ("9"). This is because these tasks lie on the critical path. The time that you can spend on your project is bound to be limited and you must therefore consider the effect of these restrictions on the completion time of the project. In other words, the assumption of unlimited resources has to be replaced with a realistic estimate of the time that you can spend on the project.

The actions that you need to take in completing a project network are summarised in figure 2.7.

1. Draw network diagram showing task identifiers, durations and interdependencies.

2. Calculate earliest event times.

3. Calculate latest event times.

4. Calculate event float.

5. Identify the critical tasks on the network.

Figure 2.7 Network action checklist

Resource chart

You can investigate the effect of resource restriction by using a resource chart. The resource chart consists of two parts, the resource bar diagram and the resource histogram. A resource chart for the worked example is shown in figure 2.8. The horizontal axis of the chart represents project weeks. Initially, it should be assumed that you can spend one day per week working on your project. You should draw this axis to allow the project plan to extend beyond the project duration that you have calculated using the network as this assumes that you have unlimited time for the project. In the worked example,

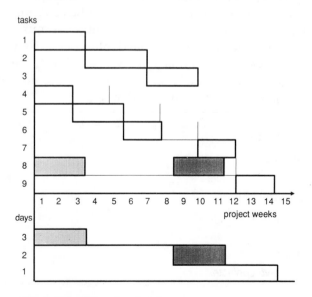

Figure 2.8 Resource chart

49

the axis is extended to 15 weeks. The vertical axis of the chart has two uses. For the resource bar diagram, it is used to identify the tasks included in the network and for the resource histogram, it represents the total number of required project work days per project week.

You must now draw the vertical axis for both parts of the chart. Having now established the resource chart framework, you can now map your project onto it. For each task that you have identified on the vertical axis of the resource bar diagram, draw a horizontal line beginning at the earliest time for the start event and ending at the latest time for the finish event. In the worked example, task 5, code program B has an earliest time for the start event of 2.2 and a latest time for the finish event of 7.2. Therefore, a horizontal line beginning at 2.2 and finishing at 7.2 is drawn. For each task, draw a bar on its horizontal line starting at the beginning of the line. The length of the bar represents the duration of the task. For task 5, the bar is 2.9 in length. For critical tasks, the bar will fill the line completely, whilst for none critical tasks there will be space on the line as is the case for task 5.

This space on the horizontal line is important because it represents the float that you have in starting and finishing tasks. When there is a resource limitation, you can often use this float to overcome the problem without having to extend the project duration. The resource histogram is used to identify resource problems. You draw the histogram by first counting the maximum number of tasks that you have to undertake during each project week. This number represents the number of project days that you have to work in the particular week. Now plot out the histogram. In the worked example, you will see that three days is required for the first three weeks, then two days for the next five weeks and finally, one day for the remaining six weeks.

---

1. Decide upon axes values.
2. Draw resource chart framework.
3. Enter the horizontal task lines.
4. Draw the task bars on the horizontal lines.
5. Total number of project days per week.
6. Draw resource histogram.
7. Identify any resource conflicts.
8. Use the resource chart to resolve conflicts.

Figure 2.9 Resource chart action checklist

The problem arises when you cannot allocate the number of specified days to the project in a given week because of other commitments. For example, suppose that you can only spend a maximum of two days per week on your project. In the example, there would be a resource conflict for the first three weeks because three project days are required. This can be overcome by using the float associated with task 8. and moving the start time for this task to week 8. This means that two days are now required for the first eleven weeks and one day is required for the remaining three weeks. Thus the conflict is resolved without having to extend the project duration. Some resource conflicts cannot be resolved in this way and you will then have to extend the project duration. You can use the resource chart to decide which tasks have to be rescheduled and by how much the project has to be extended.

The actions that you need to follow in order to create a resource chart and then to use it to identify and resolve resource conflicts are summarised in figure 2.9. Having now established a plan, you must get agreement from all those concerned with the project as to whether the plan is feasible and whether it will enable you to meet the project's objectives. This agreement should also include the occurrence of check points to review your progress.

Planning a project can be time consuming but it is essential if you are going to reduce the risk of encountering fundamental problems towards the end of the project when there will be insufficient time left to follow an alternative course of action. Remember that planning will help you understand the true nature of the work to be undertaken, it will allow you to make realistic estimates of the time and effort required and finally, it will allow you to decide upon the best sequence of performing the required work.

Control

You need to monitor your performance in order to review the feasibility of your plan on an ongoing basis. Your plan forms the basis of control and in turn, control will serve as a trigger for a replanning exercise. You must be able to measure actual progress, to identify any deviation from your plan and to indicate the necessary corrective action if you are to maintain effective control of your project. The use of a monitoring sheet together with a periodic progress report should simplify the controlling process.

Monitoring sheet

You will spend some time devising your network diagram and resource chart. Once the project starts, it will be time consuming to keep updating these documents. For the purpose of ongoing monitoring you will find it easier to transfer the key data from these documents to a monitoring sheet. You will only need to update the network diagram and resource chart when major changes take place that affect task interdependencies. All minor changes and actual progress that you make can be recorded on the monitoring sheet.

The monitoring sheet is similar to the bar chart section of the resource chart except it does not show free float and allows both amendments to be made and progress to be recorded. Each row represents a single work element, while each column represents a project week. First you must draw the planned start and finish events in the correct columns, joining each pair with a horizontal line to represent each work element. Then mark the check points for the project where you will review the project with your project supervisor and client. As your project proceeds, you can record progress by filling in the event symbols to indicate an event is complete or by drawing a vertical line in the event symbol and redrawing that symbol in another column to represent a rescheduling of the event.

An example of a monitoring sheet for the worked example is shown in figure 2.10. This shows the state of the project at week 5. You will see that task 1 has been completed, task 2 has been started, task 4 although completed took an extra week and this has had a knock on effect on task 5 which has been started but the scheduled finish has been moved to week 6.

Periodic progress report

You will have to report progress to your project supervisor and client. It is important that this procedure concentrates on the key issues and that it requires the minimum of effort on your part. The periodic progress report should help you in this reporting activity. The report gives a summary of the overall project status at a given point of time

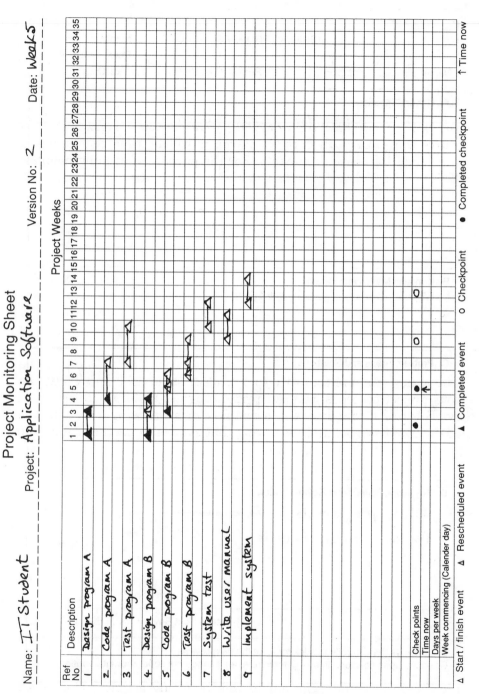

Figure 2.10 Monitoring sheet

53

PERIODIC PROGRESS REPORT   Number: ..2..

Date: Week 5

Name: IT Student   Project: Application Software

A. Current Situation

Project on schedule. Client happy with program I/o interface.

B. Contacts Made (with dates)

Project client (week 2 & 3)

C. Problem Areas and Solutions

Design problems with program B has caused some delay. Saw tutor for advice. Knock on effect localised.

D. Key Work During Next Review Period

Finish program B code and test

Finish program A code

Date of Next Review Week 9

D. becomes the control yardstick for A. at the next review.
C. encourages solutions to be put forward even if it requires supervisor intervention.

Figure 2.11 Periodic progress report

(usually a check point). There are three sections; current situation, problem areas and key work during next period.

In the current situation section, you should describe the work that you have completed since the last review together with a resume of the main issues of the project to date. In the problem areas and solutions section, you must describe the critical factors that will affect the meeting of target dates. This acts as an early warning system and focuses attention on the matters requiring urgent attention. You should also try to suggest a solution to the problem even if this requires action beyond your control. In the key work during next period section, you should list the work elements that you expect to be concentrating on during the next period. A completed report for the worked example is shown in figure 2.11.

The control of your project is vital in achieving a successful outcome. There are two main purposes of control. Firstly, it is to highlight the need for a revision of the plan either to correct some deviation or to take into account a change in project direction which has led to a change in the terms of reference. Secondly, it is to inform all interested parties of the current project status. You need to agree the frequency of reporting with your supervisor. Normally it will be between every three and five weeks. An alternative to this approach is to study the agreed project plan and place check points so that they reflect your planned activity on the project. There would be less time between check points during periods of high activity than there would be between check points during periods of low activity.

Summary

This chapter has described a method for planning and controlling your project. Together, the various components form your project map as shown in figure 2.12. It is important to remember that planning and control are not an end in themselves and therefore you should keep time spent on these activities down to a minimum. You should concentrate on the quality of planning and control rather than the particular technique used. With this in mind, you may feel that the project which you are going to undertake is sufficiently straight forward, from a planning point of view, that you can omit the network diagram and the resource chart and develop a plan using just the

Project Map Components
Terms of reference
Work element list
Network diagram
Resource chart
Monitoring sheet
Periodic progress report

Figure 2.12 Project map

work element list and the monitor sheet. This type of change in the method of planning and control is acceptable as long as it is based on reasoned judgement and not based on an attitude of disregard for this aspect of the project. You may have access to one of the many project management software packages now available on micro computers. Whilst these packages are designed primarily to aid the management of commercial and industrial projects, it is possible to use them in the management of your project. One such package is SuperProject Expert. You will find a description of this package and how it can be used for your project in Appendix A.

The framework that you establish through effective planning and control will provide you with an opportunity of achieving the most from your project. Remember that if you fail to plan then you are planning to fail!

CHAPTER 3

"IF ONLY I HAD TIME." – Personal time management

The project that you have to complete in order to pass your course will, without doubt, occupy much of your time. Your problem is that you do not have anyone else to delegate work to and so you will have to undertake all work yourself. You are the key project resource. It is important for you to understand what results are expected by your project supervisor and project client together with what needs to be done in order to achieve these results. You have to be aware of the time commitment to the project, the likely return on your effort compared to other course assessment and the time you spend on other work and social activities.

Consider the questions in figure 3.1. How many of them apply to you? It is likely that several of them do. This is because everyone has difficulty managing their own time effectively which in turn impacts on the amount that can be achieved at work and in leisure. How often have you thought, "If only I had more time I could do this or achieve that." The skill of personal time management is in allocating the right kind of time to areas of high priority whatever these may be. In this

---

Do you have little time to pursue your pastimes?

Is your workload hard to cope with?

Do you seem to work hard for little reward?

Do you tend to put jobs off until tomorrow?

Do you spend time worrying about trivial problems?

Do you feel that events tend to control you?

Figure 3.1 Initial time related questions

chapter you will learn how, by following some simple guidelines, you can make more effective use of your time.

Time and the Project

You can waste much time on the project by not really understanding what has to be done, or by communicating badly, or by not planning. There can be differences in expectations between yourself and the project supervisor or the project client. This could arise through a lack of your understanding about the client's requirements or the client's organisational environment. It could arise through a lack of the client's understanding about the role of the project in your course. Whatever the reason, this misunderstanding will lead to much time wasting.

If you have difficulty in communicating orally or in writing then time will be wasted by the recipient of your message trying to ascertain its true meaning. If you have not planned your project then you will move from one crisis to another achieving very little but using up much time. If this is true, you probably have not planned the rest of your studies properly and so the crisis situation will escalate.

Personality

The external forces of work and people have an impact on your use of time socially and in your studies. Some of the problems described in the previous section illustrate this. Before you start considering these external forces that affect the use of your time, it is worth spending a moment considering the forces within you that dictate your attitude towards time keeping and planning. These forces help form your personality. It is your personality which guides you in the way you act. It is important to recognise your own temperament and needs when planning your work. Self awareness will help your set realistic targets, plan effective periods of leisure and undertake work at times when you are likely to achieve most.

Time Management Model

Personal time management requires you to translate your long term goals and expectations into everyday activities. This can be done using the simple time management model which is a top down approach. The model is shown in figure 3.2. Start by writing down your goals and expectations for both work and social areas. It is only when you have an idea what you want to do with your life that you can decide what to spend your time on. These key areas are the main areas within which you need to use your time and concentrate your efforts.

You should restrict the number of key areas to a maximum of nine otherwise the span will become too wide for you to keep all areas in focus. When defining key areas be brief and unambiguous. Make sure you cover all activities that you have to do whilst ensuring that key areas do not overlap. The key areas shown in figure 3.3 are typical areas for a final year computing degree student. The first four key areas are the specialist modules that the student is studying. Then the next key area is the final year project, followed by the job application key area. All social and personal items have been grouped together under the last key area. The order does not reflect priority. All key areas are important in achieving your goals and expectations.

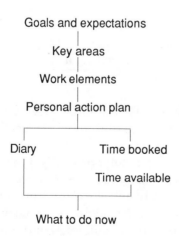

Figure 3.2 Time management model

59

1. Software engineering
2. Interactive graphics
3. Operating systems
4. Data communications
5. Final year project
6. Job applications
7. Personal and social

Figure 3.3 Example key areas for a final year computing student

You may think that examinations should be a key area. This would then cause overlap with the specialist module key areas. Revision and taking examinations are work elements of the specialist module key areas.

The work element concept was introduced in chapter two. Depending on the level of detail required, work elements are either tasks or activities. For each key area you need to decide on the level of detail and then list the work elements. There are three time dependent types of work element:

One off
These occur once only, for example, taking an examination or undertaking a fact finding interview or going to a music concert.

Adhoc recurring
These are work elements that occur more than once but the time of occurrence is irregular, for example, writing a job application form.

Regular
These recur on a regular basis, for example, attending project progress meetings or attending lectures or playing for a college team.

Decide upon the type of each work element that you have listed in the key areas. This will help when devising your personal action plan. The personal action plan is your schedule for completing work elements. It takes the form of a diary showing time booked for regular type work elements. The time left is available for the other work elements that you have listed. Decide the order of priority, the day of the week and the time of day best suited for each work element and then enter them into the diary. Do not use all the time available for listed work elements as emergencies will always arise and you will need time to cope with them. The unallocated time can then be used to complete scheduled work delayed through these emergencies.

If you want to make the most of your available time capacity, it is essential to do the large time consuming and effort demanding work elements when you are at your best. Similarly you need to save small and less demanding work for the times when you cannot reasonably do anything else. Do not be tempted to start the day by doing lots of small tasks so that they are out of the way. You will find that you break up large blocks of time during which you could have undertaken a substantial work element. It is worth identifying small tasks in your key area lists. These stand-by tasks can be done when your performance is low or there is only a small period of time available. Stand-by tasks should be done when:

either you have up to half an hour to spare,

or you do not feel like starting a large piece of work,

or the risk of interruption is great.

By maintaining a personal action plan you will find that you are concentrating your efforts on achieving your stated goals and thereby realising your expectations. You will know what to do next.

Obstacles

You will have achieved a great deal by developing a personal action plan. However, there is a potentially major problem to overcome if you are going to be effective in managing your time. The problem is that there are many obstacles which can make it very difficult to carry out your scheduled work. These obstacles fall into three groups. There are those relating to your own makeup called psychological obstacles. These will affect your attitude and motivation towards work. There are those relating to your type of study called environmental obstacles. These will affect the daily plans you have made. Finally, there are those relating to your surroundings called physical obstacles, which limit the effectiveness of your actions. Examples of obstacles are given in figure 3.4.

```
Psychological

    Lack of motivation
    Poor powers of concentration
    Indecision
    Lack of self discipline
    Inability to finish jobs

Environmental

    Poor project meetings
    Involvement in too many activities
    Too much irrelevant work
    Too much time spent reading ineffectively
    Rush jobs such as unplanned coursework

Physical

    Noisy living accommodation
    Restrictions in opening hours for library
    Poor light and or uncomfortable temperature in study areas and lecture
    theatres
```

Figure 3.4 Examples of time obstacles

The psychological obstacles can only be overcome by understanding your strengths and weaknesses and attempting to overcome the weaknesses. As mentioned earlier, it is a question of understanding your own personality. Physical obstacles can be overcome by finding a location where you can study effectively. Basically it is an area with a table and chair, fresh air, warmth and minimal distraction. The environmental obstacles can cause much time wasting and can only be overcome through careful analysis and then much self discipline in undertaking corrective action. For example, perhaps it is very tempting to go for a coffee break with a friend just after you have started a major work period but if this happens on regularly then much time can be lost. You must have the self discipline to say no if your are to overcome this obstacle.

Some obstacles can be removed as they are within your control, others will be outside your control and therefore cannot be removed. These will have to be taken into account when planning your time. By careful analysis, you should be able to identify obstacles that are wasting your time. Start this analysis by recording exactly what you do during each day for a week. The chart in figure 3.5 will assist you in recording. For each activity, record the time in minutes spent on the activity, key words describing the activity, which key area (if any) the activity is associated with and any ideas for improvement in effectiveness. At the end of the week, total up the time spent on each key area. Typically, for a student who has identified the seven key areas given in figure 3.3, the time allocation might be:

total time available: 7 days of 15 hours		105.0 hours	100%
key area 1	Software engineering	6.5 hours	6%
key area 2	Interactive graphics	7.0 hours	7%
key area 3	Operating systems	8.5 hours	8%
key area 4	Data communications	10.0 hours	10%
key area 5	Final year project	7.5 hours	7%
key area 6	Job applications	2.0 hours	2%
key area 7	Personal and social	39.0 hours	37%
non key area activity		24.5 hours	23%

The time spent on activities not in a key area is wasted time. In the example, 23% of available time has been wasted. The activities within this category are time wasters and you should investigate how you can overcome these obstacles. Use the last column on the daily time analysis chart to record your ideas for improvement.

Visual Memory

If you are going to be effective in managing your time it is important to have a constant reminder of your goals and what you have to do to achieve them. If you cannot clearly visualise your goals and you are not constantly reminded of them, it is unlikely that you will do much about them. Work you are not reminded of will simply not get done. It is a case of "out of sight out of mind". You need a visual memory in the form of daily, weekly and termly schedules together with a list of your key areas and associated work elements. This visual memory will enable you to focus on the important things. By having this information in one place, you will have easy access to it and will be able to refer to it constantly. This together with self discipline is the key to successful personal time management.

Ideally, your visual memory should comprise a loose leaf folder containing forms on which to maintain your personal action plan and key

Daily Time Analysis Chart			day of week:		date:
time of day	no of mins	activity		key area	idea for improvement
0800					
0900					
1000					
1100					
1200					
1300					
1400					
1500					
1600					
1700					
1800					
1900					
2000					
2100					
2200					

Figure 3.5 Daily time analysis chart

area details. There are many proprietary personal time management systems available. These can be expensive. You have two alternatives; either to use a day per page diary which has a large section for notes at the back or to create your own system using copies of the forms that you will find in Appendix B. The disadvantage of using a diary is that extra pages cannot be added when required and so you will be forced to use a second volume making the system cumbersome to use. The forms in Appendix B can be used in numerous ways and should enable you to develop a system to suit your own particular requirements. There are five forms available:

the key areas form,

the work element list,

the term / year plan,

the weekly schedule,

the daily plan.

The key areas form is used to list your key areas which cover your goals and expectations. The example in figure 3.6 shows the form filled in by a final year degree student.

For each key area there must be at least one work element list. Where you require a lot of detail the lists can be structured to reflect tasks and activities. The first level list would be the task list and the second level list would be the activity list.

The work element list in figure 3.7 shows some of the tasks that have to be completed for the final year project which is key area 5 on the completed key areas form. You will find it useful to adopt a numbering system to identify each work element. Each time you create a new work element allocate the next number in ascending sequence. By using the key area number as a prefix each work element can be uniquely identified. For example, the fact finding task of the project has a unique code of 5.3, and when this task is broken into activities as in figure 3.8, activities are identified as 5.3.1, 5.3.2 and so on.

For each work element, you should enter a brief description and the due date for completion. It is likely that there will not be a single due date for adhoc recurring and regular type work . You may find it useful to include the type (O for one off, A for adhoc recurring and R for regular) as well as the date. As work is done, you can the mark it off on the list. The sight of work being marked off will be encouraging and rewarding to you.

KEY AREAS	
1	Software Engineering Option (SE)
2	Data Communications Option (Dc)
3	Operating Systems Option (OS)
4	Systems Analysis Option (SA)
5	Project
6	Job Hunting
7	Personal and Social
8	
9	
NOTES	

Figure 3.6 Example of a completed key areas form

WORK ELEMENT LIST			KEY AREA 5	
NO	DETAILS		DUE DATE / /	DONE
1	Terms of reference	O	04/01/89	√
2	Project plan	R	—	—
3	Fact finding	O	22/02/89	√
4	Detailed analysis	O	08/03/89	
5	System design	O	31/03/89	
6	Program building	O	28/04/89	
7	System test	O	05/05/89	
8	System documentation	O	05/05/89	
9	Implementation	O	26/05/09	
10	Project reporting	A	—	
11	Project viva	O	14/06/89	

Figure 3.7 Example of a completed work element list

WORK ELEMENT LIST		KEY AREA 5.3	
NO	DETAILS	DUE DATE / /	DONE
1	Interview Key people	25/01/89	√
2	Issue and collect user population questionnaire	16/02/89	√
3	Observe process	25/01/89	√
4	Document analysis	20/02/89	√
5	Collation of facts	22/02/89	√

Figure 3.8 Example of a second level work element list

68

The second level work element list in figure 3.8 shows the activities that are to be undertaken for the task of fact finding. This is the lowest level of detail you should ever go to and in many instances it will be sufficient to remain at level one. It is important to remember not to overburden yourself with too much detail. You will probably find that some of your key areas will have just level one lists, some will have level one lists with a few tasks expanded to level two lists and occasionally a key area may have each level one task expanded into level two activities.

The remaining three forms of the visual memory set will help you to devise your personal action plan. By using the term / year plan, an overall long term plan can be developed which will allocate sufficient time to your key areas. The example in figure 3.9 shows a typical plan ,which has been drawn up at the beginning of the year, for the final year student. The focus should be on key areas at this level. You should identify important milestones on this plan.

The weekly schedule in figure 3.10 shows the regular work elements that have been identified in the work element lists of the key areas in figure 3.6. By creating a similar timetable, you will be able to identify the unscheduled time available. Having done this you can then allocate this time to the remaining work elements on a daily basis. You should plan adequate time for breaks and relaxation. Remember that it is important to match the type of work you have to do to the type of time that is available so that you make effective use of this time. Therefore plan to make use of odd hours and half hours.

The daily plan is used to organise each day. The due dates on the work element lists need to be taken into account when deciding which work is to be done on which day. Major work for the day is prominent at the top of the page so you will focus you attention on the important jobs. You should use this form like a diary to enable you to schedule in lectures, tutorials, meetings, appointments and specific jobs. At the beginning of each day, review what is to be done and adjust the plan accordingly. Remember not to attempt too much as you are likely to fail and then become demoralised. The example in figure 3.11 shows a completed daily plan.

You should keep your plans and schedules accessible for constant referral and attempt to stick to them until it becomes a habit. Force yourself to use spare time on work elements related to key areas.

MONTH	WK/C / /	WK NO			
SEP					
OCT	26/09/89	1			
		2			
		3			
		4			
NOV		5	TAUGHT		
		6			
		7	COURSE		
		8			
DEC		9			
		10			
		11			
		12	READING WEEK		Board of study
JAN			HOLIDAYS		
	09/01/89	13		P	
		14		R	
FEB		15		O	
		16	TAUGHT	J	
		17		E	Project presentation
		18	COURSE	C	
MAR		19		T	
		20			
		21			
		22			
APR			HOLIDAYS		
	17/04/89	23			
MAY		24	REVISION		
		25			
		26	EXAMS		
		27			
JUN		28			
		29		PROJECT	
		30			
		31			Project viva
JUL		32			
		33			
		34			Board of study
AUG					

Figure 3.9 Example of a completed year plan

TIME	MON	TUE	WED	THU	FRI	SAT	SUN
0800							
0900	SE		Project	SA			
1000					OS		
1100	DC	DC					
1200					SA		
1300							
1400	OS	SA		SE	OUTSIDE SPEAKERS	Sports	
1500	Unstaffed lab						
1600		OS					
1700							
1800				Unstaffed lab			
1900							
2000							
2100							
2200							
NOTES	Project starts term 2, use Wednesday as reading day in term 1.						

Figure 3.10 Example of a completed weekly schedule

71

DAY: *FRIDAY*	*10* / *03* *184*

MAJOR WORK OF DAY *SA assignment for Tuesday am !*

	DAY'S WORK ELEMENT LIST
0800	*SA assignment*
0900 *See personal tutor*	*Job application letter*
1000 *OS*	
1100	
1200 *SA*	
1300 *Lunch with Anne*	NOTES
1400 *Talk by IBM on OS*	
1500	
1600 *Assignment*	
1700	
1800	DON'T FORGET
1900 *Assignment + letter*	*Ring Bob*
2000	
2100 *Union !!*	
2200	

Figure 3.11 Example of a daily plan

72

Summary

This chapter has considered the area of personal time management. The skill of good time management lies in devoting the right kind of time to the areas of high priority whatever they may be. You will find that work which you find highly interesting will inevitably maintain your motivation and concentration. This may well cause you to spend longer on this work than planned and because of this other areas will suffer. You must be aware of this trap.

The checklist in figure 3.12 provides you with a focus which will help you achieve good time management. It is a case of having the right attitude of mind together with a good methodical practice. Efficiency is doing things right whilst effectiveness is doing the right things. Time management is about balancing efficiency and effectiveness.

---

1. Draw up a fixed weekly schedule

2. Do the important and difficult tasks when you are at your best

3. Start with the most important work

4. Give the day a flying start and begin early

5. Set time limits for work elements and stick to them

6. Do not put off important but unpleasant work but put off all that is unimportant

7. Avoid interrupting yourself. Jot down a suddenly remembered job for later attention

8. Prepare so that everything you need is at hand

9. Do jobs of a similar type in sequence

10. Rest and relax before it becomes necessary

11. Do things adequately well. If there is spare time you can always go back and improve

12. Keep ideas, plans and schedules in one place by maintaining a one book visual memory

13. Periodically record and then analyse your use of time

14. Try to complete at least one major task a day

Figure 3.12 Personal time management checklist

SECTION 2

Communication

Chapter 4

"Nobody will read it anyway."

This chapter deals with how to write effective progress reports, project descriptions, user guides and product descriptions. It looks at developing structures and styles for written communications.

Chapter 5

"Unaccustomed as I am ..."

Oral presentations always appear daunting to students. This chapter discusses ways in which presentations can be improved through sound preparation.

Chapter 6

"It was working this morning!"

Giving demonstrations is often a traumatic experience. This chapter suggests how to make a demonstration successful and show the product in its best light.

CHAPTER 4

"NOBODY WILL READ IT ANYWAY."
– Report writing

Written communication is extremely important in project work. It acts as a reference point for all those associated with the project, it provides a permanent record of agreed courses of action and it is the definitive description of the finished product together with a log of modifications. In your case, these written reports are particularly important. Computer software is an intangible product which makes it very difficult to assess. Assessment will tend to be through the reports you produce supported by evidence that the software exists and works correctly. For a long period of the project the reports will be all you can show your tutor. Therefore, it is important for you to master the skill of producing good quality written reports which describe fully the various aspects of your project and which make maximum impact. Remember, nobody will want to read a badly written and badly presented document.

Why are you writing this report?

Do you fully understand the terms of reference?

What information is required from the report?

Has the reader of the report any prior knowledge the project? How will this affect your writing?

How much information on the report subject is already available and will you include any?

Figure 4.1 Preliminary questions

You must be clear about the purpose of each document that you produce. It is useful to consider the questions in figure 4.1 before you start to write any document. This will help you to clarify the task you are about to undertake. You will have to produce many documents during the project, typically these will include the following:

terms of reference,

project status reports,

interim project reports,

final project report,

system documentation,

user manual.

Do not fall into the trap of believing that documentation of the project is of secondary importance. Proper presentation is an integral part of the project. It is the documentation that is visible throughout the project's life and it is likely to be this on which you are judged. A good document should be readable, interesting and well presented. It should be no longer than is necessary.

The two major writing tasks within the project are the project report and the user manual. The project report must be a clear and accurate description of all aspects of the project. The user manual must be written so that it is easy to read and understand even for the first time user of your product. This chapter will concentrate on these two documents when considering the topic of written communication.

The writing plan

You will need to plan carefully any major writing task that has to be undertaken during the project. There are three parts to consider when planning the writing task. Firstly, you must be aware of the elements in the writing process and understand the interaction between these elements. Secondly, you must decide upon an order of writing the sections of the document that is to be created. Finally, you should decide upon some general principles of how best to tackle the writing task, taking into account your own traits and abilities.

Elements in the writing process

Writing is an iterative process; you begin with a set of rough ideas and through an extended refinement procedure transform them into a finished piece. The diagram in figure 4.2 shows the six major stages in the process. Within each stage there is an iterative process which is necessary in order to derive the end-of-stage product. You will see from the diagram that the stages are interrelated so that you can undertake the refinement process by returning to and reworking previous stages as necessary.

You must start by preparing the raw material which will involve data collection, fact finding, putting your ideas on paper and then sorting and collating this information into order. Once this material is available, you can begin writing the draft. During this stage, you should ensure that the structure is logical. Check for subjects that are out of order. Make sure that there are no duplications, that no irrelevant material is included and that no material is missing.

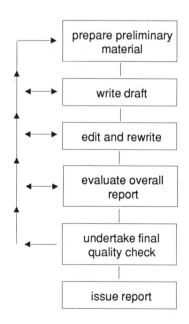

Figure 4.2 The writing process

Having got an initial draft, you can now start to refine it. The first stage is to edit and where necessary rewrite parts. Your aim at this stage is to improve the clarity and accuracy of the document. Concentrate on removing jargon and cliches, on ensuring correct grammar usage and on correcting any data or mathematical errors. Make sure that your conclusions are sound and well supported by the main body of the report. At the end of this stage you should have the basis of the final version.

The next stage is to evaluate the overall style and format. Check that the structure is acceptable and that there are no errors in section, table and illustration titles. Make sure that the numbering of sections and appendices is correct. Once you are satisfied with the overall style and format, the final quality check can be undertaken. Concentrate on reviewing the readability and consistency, making any final amendments as may be necessary. Once the report passes this final quality check it can be issued.

Order of writing

Major writing tasks during the project lend themselves to a middle-out approach. Once you have decided on the outline structure, you write the main body of the report first and add the supporting sections afterwards. The main body may cover several sections and be written over several sittings but this does not detract from the principle of the main body first and the rest later. Your document may not have to contain all the elements shown in figure 4.3 but you should be able to adapt the order of writing as given to suit your needs.

1. Finalise outline structure
2. Write main body
3. Write conclusions, recommendations and summary
4. Compile appendices and bibliography
5. Write introduction
6. Write abstract, preface and acknowledgements
7. Compile glossary of terms
8. Prepare contents list and index

Figure 4.3 Order of writing

General principles

It is worth reviewing how you undertake writing so that you can identify and adopt a practice which you feel comfortable with and which will prove successful. The general principles shown in figure 4.4 should provide you with a basis on which to build your own practice. Once you have done this, you must force yourself to adopt it until the practice becomes automatic.

In the case of your project report, you will find it easier to write sections as you proceed. At all times remember to collect rough notes for sections as these will act as prompts and will serve as the outline of what is to be written.

Writing style

You will need to adopt a particular style when writing documents associated with the project. This is because they are essentially technical documents and not literary prose of a personal or conversational nature. The tone should be impersonal. As a general rule, personal pronouns such as; I, we, you, me, my, our and us, should not appear except in quotations. Your project report is concerned with what has already been done and so it should be written in the past tense. Use active constructions rather than passive constructions as they are more forceful and save words. For example; write, "The client agreed the terms of reference." instead of,"The terms of reference were agreed by the client."

Accurate spelling is essential. Never use abbreviations, jargon, slang or cliches. Never use unnecessary multisyllabic words. For ex-

---

1. Write in as short a period as possible but take enough time to be able to compose effectively.
2. Write complete sections at single sitting.
3. If a section is broken over sittings, make notes to help effective restart4. Do not worry about style or quality, get the information down as quickly as possible, refinement and polishing can be done at the reviewing stage.
5. Have all rough notes and research material at hand before writing commences.
6. Read and revise over a period of time.

Figure 4.4 General principles

ample; "The quadriped effected its descent from the arboreal habitat in order to ingest sustenance." could be written as "The squirrel climbed down from the tree to eat." Keep your sentences short and on average 20 words long. Sentences should be grouped into short paragraphs. You will improve the clarity and readability of your documents by adopting these simple rules.

Keep the writing style checklist in mind when you are writing your reports. It will help you to establish a good working style.

Word usage

When composing you should be very aware of the words and phrases that you are using. A well constructed sentence that includes carefully chosen words will hold the reader's attention. There are some common mistakes that all writers occasionally make. You should be aware of these when writing your project documents.

There are two problems concerning the context of words. Firstly, undue repetition of a word or phrase will spoil the flow. You should avoid this and make every effort to use your favourite words sparingly. The second contextual problem concerns position. Position reflects the emphasis that you are putting on the word. Position can also transform the meaning of a sentence. For example do not write, "Only this software will run under the current operating system." when you mean "This software will only run under the current operating system."

---

1. Keep the tone impersonal

2. Use the past tense

3. Use active constructions

4. Ensure accurate spelling

5. Do not use abbreviations

6. Use short words, short sentences and short paragraphs

7. Never use jargon, slang or cliches

Figure 4.5 Writing style checklist

You should be very careful about the words you use, use standard English and avoid colloquial language and slang. Instead of writing, "The geezer hoicked the buffet down the jitty." write, "The man carried the stool along the alley." You should not use idiomatic expressions as these have special meaning that some people may not understand. Here are some examples with a better alternative.

in the pipeline	being prepared
up a gum tree	in difficulty
snail's pace	slowly
a blow below the belt	an unfair action

It is best to avoid ready made phrases as these have less impact than newly constructed ones which indicate care has been taken in composition.

Try to avoid superfluous words. Many introductory phrases and connectors can be deleted without altering the overall meaning. Circumlocution, which is the use of many words when a few would do, can reduce the quality of your work greatly. Sentences will loose sharpness and clarity. Some examples of circumlocution are give in figure 4.6.

Simplicity will help improve clarity and readability. However, in practising economy of words, do not make the mistake of using too few. Include comment words and connecting words to direct the reader's attention to key statements and to aid the flow of the report.

Project progress is reviewed on a day to day basis.

is better written:

The project is reviewed daily.

At the end of the day, there is really somewhat of an obligation upon us to look after the needs of our users.

is better written:

We ought to support our users.

At this moment in time, we are actually in the process of examining the degradation of performance of the elements of the computer equipment.

is better written:

We are examining the hardware fault.

Figure 4.6 Examples of circumlocution

Project report

Your project report is probably the most important document that you will have to produce. The material content and the presentation format will have a direct impact the perceived success or failure of your project. Your terms of reference may include details of the format and content requirements of your report. If so you must ensure you comply with these. Readers of your report will not give equal attention to all sections. You must consider which sections will receive the most attention and devote more time to these. Typically, the percentage of managers reading the sections of business reports are as follows:

Summary and abstracts	87%
Introduction	43%
Main body	12%
Conclusions and recommendations	55%
Appendices	5%

Whilst the emphasis is likely to be different for your report, there will be an imbalance in time spent on each section and therefore you should review this point carefully in order to achieve maximum impact.

Do not crowd the page and so make it unattractive and difficult to read. Make the layout clear and easy to follow. Aim for a maximum of 250 to 300 words on A4 size paper. Relevant tables, graphs, diagrams and illustrations will help you to present information quickly, clearly and concisely as well as giving the report greater appeal.

Decide upon a report format style. An example is given in figure 4.7. All headings are underlined. The chapter or section heading is centred and is in upper case. Subsections are shown as side headings with only the first letter in upper case. Sections of subsections are indented and the heading is all in lower case. There is a 4 centimetre left margin and a 2.5 centimetre right margin. This will enable the report to be bound single sided. If the report is to be bound double sided then alternate left and right margins will have to be 4 centimetres. Each page should be numbered and each chapter or section should begin on a new page.

The structure of your report will be preliminaries, followed by the main sections,followed by the addenda.

A4 paper

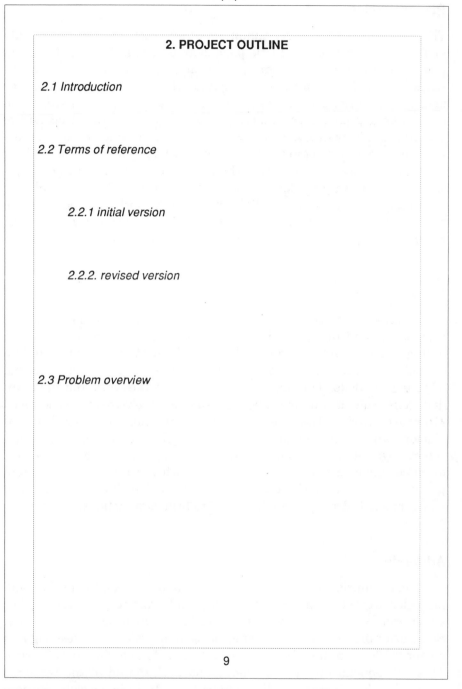

Figure 4.7 Example format of a report page

Preliminaries

These comprise title page, summary or abstract, acknowledgements and table of contents. The title page is an essential feature. It should include: the project title, your name, your course, the name of your institution and department and the date of the report. The summary or abstract is a brief and concise statement of the project; its scope, the encountered problems, the methods used and the main conclusions. Use about 200 words and be sure to make each one count. The acknowledgements recognise the people to whom you are indebted for guidance and assistance during the project. Give credit to the organisations who have provided resources during the project. The table of contents sets out the main divisions of the report and includes the page numbers. Its purpose is to provide an analytical overview of your report and to provide the reader with the sequence of presentation.

Main sections

The main sections comprise the introduction, the main body and the conclusions and recommendations. You should write the introduction with great care and aim to introduce your project in a way that arouses and stimulates the reader's interest. Write the introduction as one of your last tasks. The main body will reflect the work you have undertaken. Split the main body into sections or chapters as discussed previously. Ensure that these sections are in a logical order. The conclusions and recommendations should tie the whole project and the report together. You should restate the major points of the report, draw conclusions and leave the reader with the impressions of completeness and of a positive gain. You must not include new material which has not already been discussed in previous sections.

Addenda

Addenda comprise appendices, a glossary of terms, a bibliography and an index. Appendices contain material relevant to your report, but which would spoil the flow if it was to be included in the main body. Some examples are; a system specification, a project progress log and a user guide. You may find it beneficial to include a glossary of terms. This will depend on the knowledge and background of the intended readership. The glossary will include a list of technical words, phrases and abbreviations that you have had to use. You should include a bibliography which gives full details of all references cited in your report. The use of references will increase the credibility of your work. The inclusion of an index is only required if your report is lengthy and if readers are likely to want to dip into the report rather than reading it from start to finish.

User manual

If your project is concerned with developing a piece of software which is to be used by your project client then you will have to write a user manual. This manual should not be a comprehensive description of the software and how it works internally. It should describe the functions of the software and how it can be accessed and used. Any user manual should satisfy three aims:

to provide practical information about the software when help is not at hand,

to help inexperienced users get started quickly and with the least difficulty,

to help experienced users become productive quickly.

Before you commence writing the user manual, you should consider the following questions:

Who are the readers of the manual?

How knowledgeable are these readers?

How will the readers use the manual? Will it be from start to finish or as a reference manual or both?

Having identified your target audience and having decided what you are trying to achieve, you can now begin to write. Begin with the basic concepts. Explain why the product has been developed and what it can do for the user. Describe the primary features which are sufficient to get the user started. Base the structure of the manual on the features of the product. You can then describe each feature in a separate section, breaking it down into more detail as required. By doing this,

Begin with the basic concepts

Structure the content around the features of software

Organise logically

Make the manual completely self contained

Use examples to illustrate concepts and usage

List the error messages

Describe the common mistakes made by users

Figure 4.8 User manual checklist

you can organise the manual in a logical sequence, starting with basic points and progressing to the complex concepts and procedures. The user manual should be self contained. Therefore, you should include details of the hardware and software environment which your product needs in order to function. Wherever possible use examples to illustrate you descriptions.

Make these examples meaningful and not too complex. Include screen dumps of input and output so that the user has an exact replica of real operations. You must make sure that all your examples do work in practice. Include a list of all error messages that can be issued together with some further explanation of what each message means and how the error can be rectified. A list of common mistakes made by users is a worthwhile addition to your manual. Include the reasons why these mistakes are likely to happen and explanations of how they can be overcome.

Summary

During the project you will be required to write reports which will contribute to your assessment. Therefore, it is essential that you can write good reports. You must view writing as an integral part of your project and not regard it as an onerous chore that is to be endured and left until the end.

Use the checklist in figure 4.9 to review the effectiveness of your reports. Remember that your project is assessed and not weighed.

1. Is the report arranged logically so that the basic message and main topics emerge?

2. Is the style and presentation suited to the subject matter and the readers?

3. Have you avoided the use of generalisations?

4. Have you used technical language which might be unfamiliar to the readers?

5. Have you avoided the use of slang, cliches, colloquialisms and idioms?

6. If special terminology is unavoidable, have you provided suitable explanations?

7. Is any of the information more suitable for presentation in graphs, tables or diagrams?

8. Are the preliminaries in the correct sequence, in the correct format and complete?

9. Is the main section carefully organised and consistent with the table of contents?

10. Does the main section include a good introduction and a carefully reasoned conclusion which includes no new material?

11. Is the main section unnecessarily cluttered or have appendices been used effectively?

12. Are the appendices referred to in the main section and if not are they warranted?

13. Is there a suitable bibliography?

14. Is the report suitably formatted with margins headings and sub-headings?

15. Have the requirements of your clients been checked regarding format and presentation?

Figure 4.9   Report writing checklist

CHAPTER 5

"UNACCUSTOMED AS I AM ..."
– Oral presentations

At some stage during the project, you will probably have to give a presentation which covers the progress that you have made to date and the product that you are developing. You may have to give a presentation on more than one occasion. It is important that you become comfortable with delivering presentations as the impression you give at them can greatly influence the view people have of your project and therefore the overall assessment of your work.

You must be clear as to the objective of your presentation. Is it an opportunity for your assessors to question you about the project report that you have already distributed? Is your presentation the vehicle you are to use in explaining how you have undertaken the project work? Is your talk meant to consolidate your report and highlight the key issues? Whatever the objective, make sure you fully understand what you are expected to present. By doing this you will be more likely to concentrate your efforts on the main theme and you will be able to review the material you wish to present , placing it in order of importance with respect to the presentation objective. This last point will help you to cut down your material without losing any key details as you will usually find that you will have more than enough material for the time available.

Always remember that you are attempting to inform your audience about your project and persuade them that it is a quality piece of work. Your presentation should be balanced in every respect:

not too short but not too long,

not too formal but not too informal,

not too much content but not too little content,

not over prepared but not under prepared.

You should aim to be natural, to gain and maintain your audience's attention and to present the key issues effectively.

When preparing and giving your talk bear in mind the pointers shown in figure 5.1. These should act as triggers to the major issues that you should address if you are to deliver a polished and effective performance.

The Audience

The first matter that you should consider when preparing your presentation is your audience. Whilst it is reasonable to assume that some may be conversant with the general subject area of the project, it is unreasonable and even foolish to assume that all your audience will have an in depth knowledge of the subject area and that they all have some prior knowledge of your project. If possible, try to ascertain who will be in the audience beforehand so that you can tailor the format and content to suit. Your audience is likely to be a small group of no more than ten people and so, compared to a much larger group, it should be easier to build a rapport with them and to keep the proceedings relatively informal. Whatever is to follow, make sure that your opening remarks are stimulating and gain the audiences attention. Once an audience's interest is lost, it is very difficult to regain it. Remember that audiences are people. They want to be entertained. Speak to them and not at them. Look at them all but avoid staring at one particular section.

Understand the objectives of your talk

Plan your talk

Know your audience

Prepare properly

Know your subject thoroughly

Practice your talk before hand

Deliver your talk with confidence

Figure 5.1 Initial pointers for presentations

Audiences are people
Talk to them and look at them
React to the mood of your audience
Do not belittle members of the audience
Do not presume knowledge of the subject area and your project
If your make a mistake or go wrong, apologise and correct the error
Be sensitive to your audience

Figure 5.2 Audiences

Presentation Format

Your presentation should have a beginning, a middle and an end. Carefully plan what each section is to contain so that you can achieve maximum impact. Having decided on the content, you can then consider how you are going to present the material in terms of the style you are going to adopt and the visual aids that you are going to use.

The beginning is very important. You need to gain your audiences attention quickly and make a good first impression. Tell them what you are going to speak about and outline the format of your talk. Decide when you will answer questions and consequently, invite your audience to ask questions either at the end or as and when they occur. Leaving questions until the end is probably the safer course of action as interruptions can cause you to loose your train of thought and become sidetracked. Depending on the content and format of your talk, it may be useful to mention where further information can be obtained. This may be from prepared handouts, or from the project report, or by attending a demonstration session, or by running a demonstration disk. Demonstrations are covered in Chapter 6. Above all, make some initial remarks which arouse the audience's interest.

The main body of your talk should be used to present your case in a clear and logical manner. Each point should lead naturally onto the next. Ensure that you stress the key points both verbally and visually. At the end of each major point, summarise the topic before moving on. You can clarify and emphasise points through using examples or illustrations or, if your project includes a demonstration of the product prior to the presentation, by referring to this demonstration.

Beginning	SAY WHAT YOU WILL SAY
Middle	SAY IT
End	SAY WHAT YOU HAVE SAID

Figure 5.3 Presentation format

At the end of your talk, you should briefly recap the points made. This will help to reinforce the message of your talk. It will ensure that you have not omitted any important point. It will help those in the audience who may have missed something to understand fully. Do not use the end section to introduce new ideas or material. Once you have answered questions and thanked your audience for their attention, finish with a clear message that they will remember and be impressed by.

The format of your presentation should be simple as shown in figure 5.3. You will then be able to convey your message more easily, more clearly and with greater impact.

Using Visual Aids

Evidence exists which shows that people retain only 10% of what they hear but when information is supported visually, the retention rate is increased to 50%. Studies show that visuals help to influence decisions and assessment. It has been found that presenters using visuals win their points 67% of the time which is about twice as often as those not using them. Relate this to your project and you will see that it is worthwhile producing and using good quality visuals for your presentation. Your chance of success and of creating a good impression will be increased.

You must first decide which type of visual you are going to use in your presentation. Remember that using a black board or a white board has some serious disadvantages. You must create your visuals during the presentation and for this you will have to turn your back on the audience. There will be a temptation to talk while creating and this is poor delivery technique. It will take time to create these visuals, your time will be restricted and may be better spent talking to your audience. Lastly, it takes practice to write well on these boards and you may find that the results you achieve degrade rather than enhance your presentation. Perhaps you should play safe and use overhead projector foils which you can prepare beforehand.

You can achieve some impressive results using an overhead projector, if you follow some simple guidelines when creating your foils.

General procedure

Once you have prepared your notes for your presentation, work through them marking those points which you wish to reinforce visually.

Decide how each point is to be represented; in words, by a picture, by a diagram or by using combination of both words and pictures.

Limit the information on your visuals to the key points. This will involve summarising text and simplifying pictures and diagrams.

Decide upon a general format for your visuals which promotes continuity and uniformity within your set of foils. You must ensure that the material on each visual links to the next and supports what you are going to say. In this way, your message will be reinforced.

Now produce your visuals.

Production of visuals

Each visual should contain only one idea. A good visual will contain only the key information displayed in a way which makes it easy to comprehend. If you find that the single idea for a given visual requires detailed information then format the visual so that you can display the information in stages using a card mask to reveal the next stage.

Make sure that each visual is accurate which includes being free of spelling mistakes, containing correct information and not emphasising unimportant points.

Each visual should be as brief as possible so that the contents can be quickly assimilated and the information is retained as long as possible. Approximately 40 to 50 words can be absorbed in one go, so try to keep within this limit for each visual. If you intend to write further information onto a visual during your presentation take this into account during the production process.

Pictures and diagrams should be simple outlines. All lines should be bold (1.5mm wide) as faint lines are likely to disappear when projected.

The normal size of the area that can be projected on an overhead projector is a square of 25cm. It is important to use this effectively.

Words and pictures should be as large as possible to make sure that they are easily visible. Make sure that the layout is well formatted and that the information is logically grouped on the visual.

The actual letter size should be a minimum of 6mm for upper case letters. The corresponding minimum for lower case letters will be slightly smaller. This minimum will allow an audience to read your visuals comfortably at 6m. Lower case letters are easier to read than upper case, so use them for the main part of text and use upper case for titles or for emphasis. Leave slightly more space between letters than if you were printing on to paper.

Do not place the lines too close together otherwise the words will be difficult to read. As a guide, leave at least 1cm between lines. You can create a structure by leaving more space between blocks of lines.

Align your text from the left hand side. Do not try to centre text as this can often look untidy and can be distracting.

Emphasise important points by using, upper case letters, or different size letters, or underlining or colour. The point of maximum visual impact is just above centre. Wherever possible, try to format your visuals so that this is the position where the most important piece of information on each visual are located.

Colour can be used to good effect. You can use it to attract attention, to highlight important information, to aid identification, to colour code flow paths on a diagram, or to create a structure for a visual. Colour can be used as a background, to make viewing more comfortable. Use colours which are vivid and contrasting but be aware that the use of too many colours on a visual can become distracting.

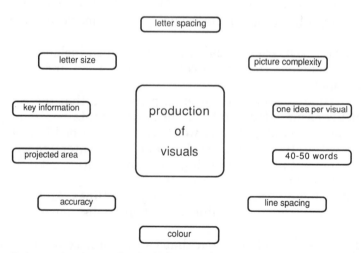

Figure 5.4 Pointers for the production of visuals

If you are going to hand write your visuals they must be neat and tidy. Letters should be bold and legible. You can keep letters straight by writing along a ruler.

It is worth spending time on producing high quality visuals for your presentation. By following the simple guidelines, you will be able to produce some good results. Remember this final piece of advice:

A GOOD VISUAL IS:

BIG and BOLD

CLEAR and CONCISE

STIMULATES INTEREST

ATTRACTS ATTENTION

GETS THE MESSAGE ACROSS

Distractions

If your presentation is to be effective, you must stop your audience's attention wandering and ensure that they receive the message that you are attempting to convey. Distractions must be avoided as they will distort your message, make the task of presenting more difficult and increase the time that you need to convey the information. The common distractions are:

indistinct or illegible visuals,

a speaker who talks to the visuals or mumbles,

a speaker who stares at one section of the audience,

a speaker who gesticulates wildly,

redundant or irrelevant information,

sidetracking from the main point,

poor timekeeping,

internal or external noises.

You must be aware of possible distractions and take the necessary steps to overcome them as they occur.

Administrative Details

The environment in which your presentation takes place will have a considerable effect on the success or failure of your talk. Whilst there will be aspects of the room, its layout and the equipment available that you may not have control over, there will be many aspects that you can control to ensure that the environment is as supportive as possible to your delivery.

There are three major administrative points to consider, the seating arrangement for the audience, where you should be located and the equipment that you have at your disposal.

You should make sure that the room layout will enable everyone to see the screen and that you can present you work in comfort. Seating is best arranged in either a horseshoe or in a classroom style. If you are going to use an overhead projector, the screen should be higher than the audience's heads and angled to reduce problems of reflections and to reduce the likelihood of you obstructing the audience's view.

Position yourself in front of your audience so that you have easy access to your visual aids. It is probably best to stand. If a lecturn is available, use this to place you notes on for prompting. If one is not available then, it is best to hold your notes rather than leave them on a table as this will cause you to look down too much instead of looking at your audience. If you plan to write on foils or a flip chart or a white board or a black board take into account whether you are left or right handed. For ease of writing and reduced obstruction of the audience's view stand to the left of the visual you are going to write on (when facing the visual) if you are right handed and to the right if you are left handed. Two examples of room arrangements are given in figure 5.5. The examples are for a right handed presenter who is going to use an overhead projector and a black board.

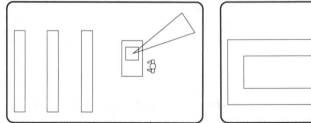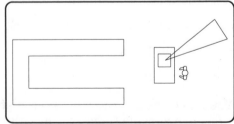

Figure 5.5 Possible room arrangements

The equipment that is likely to be available to you for you talk has already been itemised. If you are using an overhead projector make sure that it is in working order and that it is properly focused before you start.

You may be considering using a computer during you talk to illustrate certain aspects of your project. Your audience will find it difficult to see detail on the screen and unless you have access to a special attachment which enables the computer screen image to be projected using an overhead projector it may prove impractical to use the computer in your talk. Remember that there is likely to be a demonstration session for your project which will provide a better opportunity to use the computer in support of your case.

Be prepared for the unexpected, a bulb may blow, or you may not have planned to write on a visual but find you have to in order to answer a question, or you may find that the heat from the projector is curling your foils. It is useful to have some support materials available in these situations. The presentation tool kit in figure 5.6 lists those items that you may have to use during your talk. Use this list as a starting point from which to devise your own tool kit.

Coloured pens for OHP foils, flip chart and white board

Chalk for black board

Blank OHP foils

Weights to prevent foils curling

Spare OHP bulb

Pointer

Stiff card to mask foil contents

Cloth or board rubber

Presentation notes

Audience handouts

Figure 5.6 Presentation tool kit

The Delivery

Your preparation is now complete and the moment of truth has arrived, it is time to deliver your presentation. You need to convince your audience that your project has been successfully completed. To achieve this, your presentation should be persuasive. If you have done your preparation properly then the presentation structure and content should form a logical case. This is one element of the persuasive presentation. The other element is emotion. You need to be enthusiastic towards your project and deliver your argument with confidence. Your audience is then more likely to believe in you and your project and so support your cause.

Speak clearly, so that all your audience can hear. You must never mumble. Pause to allow a point to sink in or to emphasise a point. There is no need to rush from one point to another fearing that a break indicates that you are floundering. Whilst you must never rush, it is worthwhile varying your pace as this will make your presentation more interesting. Pitch is equally important. A varied pitch will add to the interest level of your talk.

When you are using visual aids, give your audience time to digest them before moving on. Once you have used a visual aid discard it, otherwise it will be distractive. So turn over flip charts, clean boards and switch off the projector.

Avoid odd mannerisms that draw your audience's attention away from your message. Whilst it is unwise to stand rigidly to attention, it is equally unwise to wander around restlessly or gesticulate wildly. You should use action to emphasise the important points.

You should avoid reading from a prepared script because this type of presentation is usually dull and unconvincing. The notes that you use should comprise very short simple phrases which will remind you of the subject matter, the visual aid cues and method of delivery of a point. Keep these notes simple, clear and large as you will only be able to glance at them occasionally.

Summary

You may not have given any presentations before. It can be a terrifying experience but it does not have to be. You can succeed if you recognise that a large proportion of the success can be attributed to practice and being prepared. Always remember that you are trying to convey a message to an audience who might not have an in depth knowledge of your project and so the presentation must be clear and concise. Always remember the golden rule in figure 5.7 when you are giving a presentation.

Your presentation will have a significant effect on the likely success of your project, it is an opportunity for you to demonstrate your understanding of the project problem and your ability to solve this problem. Remember that you will never get a second chance to create a good first impression so make sure your talk is the best you can deliver.

MAKE IT SIMPLER
complexity is the enemy
of comprehension

Figure 5.7 The golden rule

CHAPTER 6

"IT WAS WORKING THIS MORNING!"
– Demonstrations

If your project is concerned with the development of a piece of software, then as part of your assessment you are likely to be asked to demonstrate it. This demonstration will enable your tutor and your client to assess the quality and completeness of your product. Before you start your preparation, make sure that you clearly understand the objectives of giving the demonstration.

Audience

Who is to attend your demonstration will have a direct bearing on the format and content of it. A large group of people are more likely to have a wider range of interests and reasons for attending than a small group. Therefore, the demonstration to a large group will be more generalised and more high level than that to a smaller group when the interests can be identified and the demonstration tailored accordingly.

There are two distinct courses of action you can take. One is to overview a large area of your product and the other is to choose a single aspect of your product and to demonstrate this in detail. To help you decide which is the best course of action you must try to assess the composition of the intended audience and in particular the cognitive styles of the individuals. Your audience is more likely to react favourably to your demonstration if it is consistent with the audience's overall cognitive style. The main points to take into account are:

Perception and the way of thinking: Some people find it easier to handle summarised information while others prefer a lot of detail. Some people like to consider complex problems as wholes, others prefer to divide them into simpler sub-problems.

The data: There are those who can view data realistically only in the context of its environment, while others can view data realistically even when its is independent and isolated from its context.

The vehicle of thought: Some people use abstract models to solve problems by inputting real data into a model and observing the model's performance. Others rely on experience and common sense to solve problems by relating current situations to similar experiences of the past.

By observing the characteristics of the individuals in your target audience, you should be able to adapt the format and content of your demonstration so that it appears as attractive to them as possible.

Physical factors

The physical layout of the demonstration area will impact on the success of your demonstration. Obviously, the number of people attending is a crucial factor. For an audience greater than four, you will have to consider using more than one monitor because it will be very difficult for people to see the details on the screen. The options are:

to use a slave monitor as a repeater,

to use a larger screen monitor,

to use a device which enables the computer screen images to be projected on to a screen using an overhead projector,

to hold more than one demonstration so no more than four attend.

The option you choose will depend upon the resources that are available to you. Remember to book scarce resources well in advance so that you can achieve maximum impact during the demonstration.

The positioning of equipment and the location of your audience and yourself relative to the equipment are all important. Arrange the screen so that there are no bright lights reflected on it when viewed by the audience. Make sure that there are no distractions in the audience's field of vision, for example bright lights behind the screen, windows with interesting views behind the screen and sunlight in the faces of the audience. Be careful to position yourself so that you can see the screen and operate the keyboard but that you do not obstruct the audience's view. You should make sure that the screen is sharp, that there is no grime or finger marks on the screen and that individual characters can be easily read and do not flicker or move.

Demonstration format

Like all forms of presentation, your demonstration should have a beginning, a middle and an end. You are likely to have a limited period of time and so you have to ensure that you use it effectively. A thirty minute demonstration should give you sufficient time to demonstrate the main features of your software.

The structure and content will vary depending on your product and your audience. Keep your introduction short and use it to explain what and how you are going to demonstrate your product. Use the majority of your time for the main body, leaving some time at the end for your concluding remarks. The demonstration will probably be an informal affair and certainly less formal than your presentation. You must be prepared for interruptions by members of the audience who wish further explanation or require you to go into more detail about a certain aspect of your product. Use these situations to your advantage by structuring the demonstration so that it will guide and encourage your audience to interrupt and ask questions about the strengths of your software and not the weaknesses. A simple ploy is to make an aside, which is likely to invoke questions, about a particular good feature of your software but do not demonstrate it. Your audience will do the rest!

You must decide whether you are going to give a rolling demonstration or an interactive demonstration. A rolling demonstration is one which is pre-staged where all the responses are set up beforehand and so the routes through the product are predetermined. You will have to prepare a special version of the software for this mode of demonstration. During the presentation you explain what each screen is demonstrating and then press a key to move to the next screen. This type of demonstration does not allow for any side tracking or rerouting during the presentation. You may find this a useful mode to use if your product is not very resilient, or if you have built a prototype which has some lower level modules missing that have been simulated, or if your product has a very complex range of facilities of which you only wish to demonstrate the major ones in the time available.

The second mode is the interactive demonstration in which you use the production version of your software. It is your task during the demonstration to pick the facilities, to input the correct data and to activate the generation of results. This mode will allow you to alter what you had originally planned to demonstrate based on the audience's questions. It provides you with flexibility but you have to be fully conversant with all the facilities of your product so that there are no long pauses in the proceedings as you struggle to recollect how to activate a particular feature. You must also be aware of the possibility of being side tracked into troubled waters. You may find this is a useful mode to use if your product does not lend itself to the specification of predefined routes. For example; it is much easier to develop a rolling demonstration for an accounts package than it is for a word processing package. You may feel that all the features of your product can be demonstrated in the time available and so it would be a waste of effort to develop a special rolling version. Finally, you may have restrictions placed on you by your assessors which means the production version has to demonstrated.

Many proprietary software products have demonstration versions available for evaluation purposes. Many of these can be obtained free of charge. Before you decide upon the structure and content of your demonstration, obtain some of these demonstration disks and see how the software vendors have attempted to promote the best features of their products.

Whichever type of demonstration you choose, it is important that the data used is meaningful and realistic. This will enhance the quality and clarity of the demonstration. It will enable your audience to comprehend quickly the true value of the product that you have developed.

Contingencies

Demonstrations go wrong and yours will be no exception. You must plan for this likelihood and have contingencies ready. Start by compiling a list of things you think might go wrong. Then decide how likely it is that these will occur. It will be sufficient to classify potential disasters as having a high, medium or low likelihood of occurring. You can then concentrate on those problems that have the highest probability of occurring and decide what course of action you will take if they occur. A typical list is shown in figure 6.1. The solutions that you decide upon must be realistic and effective. Try to arrive at solutions which can be used for more than one disaster.

Allow plenty of time immediately before your demonstration starts so that you can get organised and can load your software onto the computer. Better the disasters happen before your audience arrives than when they are present. You will then have a chance to overcome the problem, to reorganise the planned format and content and to compose yourself again.

Documentation and handouts will prove useful support aids during your demonstration. They will help you to overcome disasters and to answer questions.

DISASTER	LIKELIHOOD of OCCURRENCE	SOLUTION
no printer or printer failure	medium	use hard copy samples
computer malfunction	medium	use spare computer or reschedule event
disk failure	high	use backup disks
software error	high	reload software or skip facility but always apologise
power failure	low	use hard copy samples or reschedule event

Figure 6.1 A demonstration disaster plan

Handouts might include:

product summary,
function checklists,
sample reports,
screen dumps,
file capacity details.

Documentation that should be available should include:

software specifications,
program listings,
user guide,
project report.

The documentation will not be referred to in detail. Its main purpose is to add weight and credibility to your demonstration.

Summary

Your demonstration is the time when you will be expected to show that your product does work and that it meets the agreed terms of reference. Time will be limited, so you must plan to use this time very carefully. Do not assume that everything will go as planned. Have contingencies in place for likely disasters. Always have something extra to demonstrate should time permit or in response to audience questions. Remember to demonstrate to the strengths and not the weaknesses of your product. Never knock your product someone else will try to do that!

SUMMARY

Chapter 7

"House of cards"

"HOUSE OF CARDS"

Your project is one of the most challenging parts of your course. It is vitally important to be able to apply the skills and techniques that you have learnt on your course. Your project will give your a great opportunity to practise this application. In order for you to gain the most out of this opportunity you must organise yourself in an effective manner.

Chapter 2 has provided you with a method of planning your project. Use the components of the project map to achieve the appropriate level of project management. It is important to remember that project planning and control are not an end in themselves and therefore you should keep the time spent on these activities to a minimum. Concentrate on achieving quality in these activities.

Your time is at a premium. There are many calls on your time. You must manage your time effectively if you are going to achieve the best possible results in attending your course. The skill lies in devoting the right kind of time to the areas of high priority. Chapter 3 has described the common problems associated with personal time management and has provided you with a simple method for managing you own time effectively.

Your technical and management abilities will count for nothing unless you can convey your results to the assessors of your project. A piece of software is an intangible product which is difficult to assess. For a large part of the project, you will be assessed on what you report either orally or in writing. Whilst many people do not enjoy report writing or giving presentations, it is a very important element of every project. A technically sound project can be failed through the student being unable or unwilling to communicate to those assessing the work. You must devote sufficient time to this crucial project element.

Written communication acts as a reference point for all those associated with the project. It provides a permanent record of the agreed course of action. It is the definitive description of the finished product and describes the methods used in undertaking the work. The key issues that need to be addressed have been covered in Chapter 4.

You will inevitably have to give a presentation at some point during your project. With thorough preparation and practice you will be able to create a good impression with your audience. Chapter 5 has described the structure a presentation should take. You have been provided with pointers on producing good support visuals and on how to deliver you talk. If you know your subject thoroughly and you have prepared properly then you can be confident in presenting the material to your audience.

If your project involves the creation of a piece of software, then it is likely that you will be asked to demonstrate it as part of the project assessment. It is the time when you will be expected to show that your product does work and that it does meet the agreed terms of reference. Chapter 6 has given you some guidelines for demonstrating software. Always demonstrate to the software's strengths and always have something in reserve.

Usually, projects fail not because of one single major catastrophe but through a combination of poor work practices and poorly executed techniques. Take some cards away from a house built of cards and it will come tumbling down. If you do not address the management and communication elements as well as the technical element of your project then, just like the house of cards, it will come tumbling down and you will fail the project and probably the course that you are attending.

DON'T LET IT HAPPEN TO YOU!

APPENDICES

APPENDIX A

Using SuperProject Expert for student projects

SuperProject Expert is a micro computer based project management software package from Computer Associates. The package supports a range of project management techniques which simplify the scheduling, costing, reporting and updating of simple and complex projects. It enables project work elements (or tasks in SuperProject Expert terminology) to be defined and the interrelationships between work elements to be defined, specifying the duration of each work element, when work elements must start or finish and what resources work elements require. Having defined the project, it is then possible to evaluate the feasibility of the project schedule. Once a feasible scheduled is derived this can be used as a base against which to monitor actual progress, highlighting the need for corrective action when actual progress falls short of planned progress.

SuperProject Expert's features which are of particular relevance to student projects include:

A choice of sequential or concurrent task dependence relationships (Finish-to-Start, Start-to-Start, Finish-to-Finish, with lead/ lag times).

Baseline scheduling for comparison of actual and planned work.

Numerous project views: Pert Charts (network diagrams in Chapter 2), Gantt Charts (including resource charts in Chapter 2), Work Breakdown Structure Outlines and Charts, Task and Resource Calendars, individual task and resource summaries.

Standard and customised reporting facilities.

User control over program functions which enables the package to be configured to meet specific operational requirements. This includes a three-level experience mode that defines the facilities available for use.

A comprehensive, context-sensitive Help facility.

A series of steps should be followed when using SuperProject Expert to plan and monitor a student project. This series is as follows:

Define the project objectives.

Define the project structure.

Define the work elements or tasks.

Estimate the task durations.

Define the task dependencies.

Identify project and resource constraints.

Establish project and resource calendars.

Create a project baseline schedule.

Track work progress.

Evaluate and adjust the project schedule.

SuperProject Expert Features

Menus

The top two lines of any SuperProject Expert screen are the menubar. The top line lists the current screen, program and current project names. The second line displays the menu names: View, Edit, Select, File, Output and Help. Each of these pull down menus comprises a set of functions some of which may invoke a second level menu which comprises another set of functions.

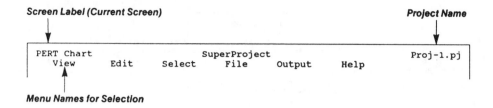

The menus are used to control and navigate through the package.

Data

Data comprises four types: project data, task data, resource data and assignment data. Data is held in data fields, if the data field is present within a view of the project then, in general, data can be input, amended or deleted from that field. This makes the package extremely powerful and flexible in the way the user can interact with it.

Outline

The Outline screen represents tasks as entries in a table. This screen is convenient for entering a large amount of data. It is also helpful when the structure of the project is being established by grouping tasks under phase headings.

Heading/Task Resource	Task ID	Pr	Dur	Dev	Schd Start	Schd Finish
SALE.PJ	P1		19	0.00	05-27-87	06-22-87
Window Displays	008		5	0.00	05-27-87	06-02-87
Clothing	001		4	0.00	05-27-87	06-01-87
Lighting	002		3	0.00	06-02-87	06-04-87
Backdrop	003		2	0.00	06-12-87	06-15-87
Display Cases	007		5	0.00	05-27-87	06-02-87
Accessories	004		8	0.00	06-02-87	06-11-87

Pert Chart

This view of the project shows each task as a box which holds the task name, the primary resource allocated to the task, the duration and the start and finish times. Tasks are linked to reflect the dependencies.

117

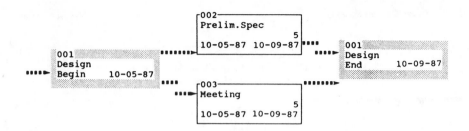

Once the tasks are created, linked in a logical order and their durations entered, the schedule can be analysed. Most projects will have several paths. SuperProject Expert highlights the critical path on the Pert Chart.

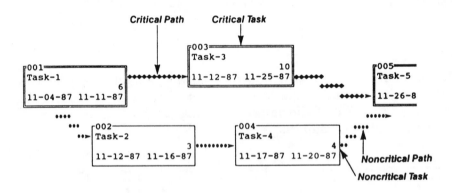

Float

There are two kinds of float in SuperProject Expert, float and free float.

Float is the number of work days a task can be delayed before it becomes a critical task, where further delay would delay the project finish date. Float includes free float.

Free float is the number of work days a task can be delayed before delaying the start of any other task.

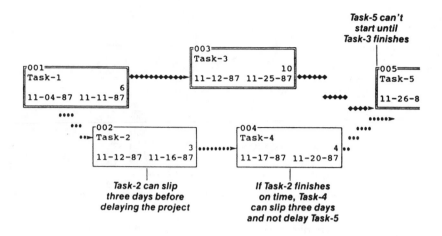

Task-5 can't start until Task-3 finishes

Task-2 can slip three days before delaying the project

If Task-2 finishes on time, Task-4 can slip three days and not delay Task-5

Task Gantt

This view shows the task relationships over time. The previous Pert Chart can be viewed as a Task Gantt.

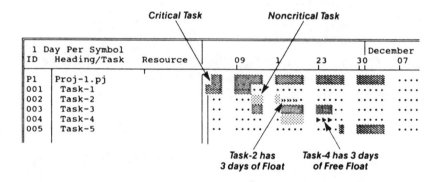

Critical Task *Noncritical Task*

Task-2 has 3 days of Float *Task-4 has 3 days of Free Float*

If task-2 slips three days, it becomes a critical task on the critical path. If task-4 slips three days, it may delay the start of the successor task, but may not necessarily delay the project finish date.

Histogram Resource Gantt

This shows the tasks a resource is allocated to over time on a Resource Gantt and the total time the resource is allocated for each work day.

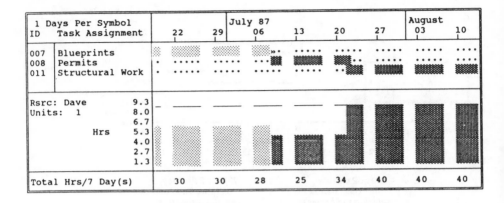

1 Days Per Symbol				July 87				August	
ID	Task Assignment	22	29	06	13	20	27	03	10
007	Blueprints								
008	Permits								
011	Structural Work								
Rsrc: Dave	9.3								
Units: 1	8.0								
	6.7								
Hrs	5.3								
	4.0								
	2.7								
	1.3								
Total Hrs/7 Day(s)		30	30	28	25	34	40	40	40

A resource conflict can occur when a resource has more work scheduled than it can perform on that day. This is highlighted on the Resource Histogram.

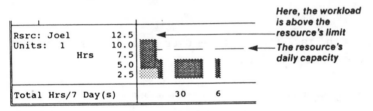

The options open to the student in this situation are either to delay specific task assignments so the workload fits within the time available or to expand the time available by working extra hours.

Calendars

SuperProject Expert's Project and Resource Calendars contain information on scheduled work days and work day lengths for the entire project and individual resources. Standard vacations can be identified as well as an individual's unavailability. The calendars can be used to define the time available for a student project that is to be done on a part time basis in parallel with other activities.

Project Baseline

SuperProject Expert can preserve the original project schedule as a Project Baseline, which can be used to measure actual performance against. As the project progresses the actual hours, actual start dates

120

and actual finish dates can be entered using the Outline screen. On the Gantt, the actuals will gradually replace the scheduled dates on the first Gantt line, while the planned dates show directly beneath.

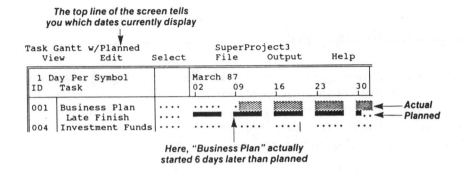

The top line of the screen tells you which dates currently display

Here, "Business Plan" actually started 6 days later than planned

The Outline screen is useful for comparing dates because, through its ability to rearrange columns of data, it is convenient for reporting.

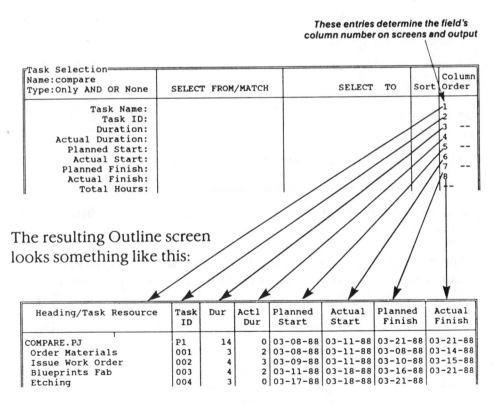

These entries determine the field's column number on screens and output

The resulting Outline screen looks something like this:

Heading/Task Resource	Task ID	Dur	Actl Dur	Planned Start	Actual Start	Planned Finish	Actual Finish
COMPARE.PJ	P1	14	0	03-08-88	03-11-88	03-21-88	03-21-88
Order Materials	001	3	2	03-08-88	03-11-88	03-08-88	03-14-88
Issue Work Order	002	4	3	03-09-88	03-11-88	03-10-88	03-15-88
Blueprints Fab	003	4	2	03-11-88	03-18-88	03-16-88	03-21-88
Etching	004	3	0	03-17-88	03-18-88	03-21-88	

By placing the planned dates next to the actual dates, a convenient work progress input and reporting screen can be created.

The Student Project

SuperProject Expert can be used to good effect in managing a student project. Once the initial burden of learning how the package works and entering the start data has been overcome, then the monitoring and rescheduling is a very easy, non-time consuming task.

The way in which the package can be used is summarised as follows:

To define project and resource constraints use CALENDARS.

To create the network of work elements with their associated attributes use PERT.

To input bulk data use OUTLINE.

To analyse student time availability and utilisation use HISTOGRAM RESOURCE GANTT.

To analyse actual performance use PROJECT BASELINE, GANTTS and OUTLINE.

A demonstration pack is available for SuperProject Expert. The pack contains:

a working version of the software with save and print inhibited,

a mini user guide for SuperProject Expert,

a demonstration of a student project together with a set of utilities for student projects.

The remaining part of this appendix provides samples of SuperProject Expert screens and reports using data for a typical student project.

Project: MY-PROJ.PJ
        Revision: 0

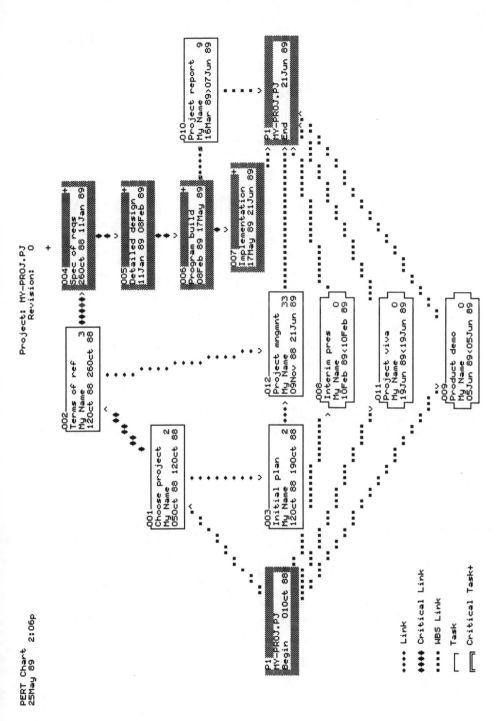

- • • • Link
- ◆◆◆ Critical Link
- ■ ■ ■ WBS Link
- Task
- Critical Task+

Heading/Task	Task ID	Pr	Dur	Schd Start	Schd Finish	Allc	Un	Total Hours	Ovr Hours	+
MY-PROJ.PJ	P1		141	05Oct 88<	21Jun 89			578	273	
‡Choose project	001		2	05Oct 88	12Oct 88			12	0	
‡Terms of ref	002		3	12Oct 88	26Oct 88			18	0	
‡Initial plan	003		2	12Oct 88	19Oct 88			12	9	
Spec of reqs	004		41	26Oct 88	11Jan 89			78	1	
‡ Fact finding	026		6	26Oct 88	17Nov 88			36	0	
‡ Modelling	027		7	17Nov 88	11Jan 89			42	1	
Detailed design	005		21	11Jan 89	08Feb 89			114	73	
‡ Input design	028		4	11Jan 89	26Jan 89			24	1	
‡ Output design	029		4	11Jan 89	26Jan 89			24	19	
‡ File design	030		6	11Jan 89	08Feb 89			36	24	
‡ Process design	031		5	11Jan 89	01Feb 89			30	29	
Program build	006		41	08Feb 89	17May 89			216	138	
‡ Build A	013		5	08Feb 89	01Mar 89			30	1	
‡ Test A	014		4	01Mar 89	16Mar 89			24	4	
‡ Link A	015		2	16Mar 89	10May 89			12	12	
‡ Build B	016		5	08Feb 89	01Mar 89			30	21	
‡ Test B	017		6	01Mar 89	10May 89			36	19	
‡ Link B	018		2	10May 89	17May 89			12	10	
‡ Build C	019		5	08Feb 89	01Mar 89			30	30	
‡ Test C	020		5	01Mar 89	12Apr 89			30	29	
‡ Link C	021		2	12Apr 89	10May 89			12	12	
Implementation	007		25	17May 89	21Jun 89			60	40	
‡ System test	022		3	17May 89	31May 89			18	14	
‡ User training	023		2	17May 89	24May 89			12	12	
‡ Data loading	024		4	31May 89	21Jun 89			24	8	
‡ Installation	025		1	31May 89	31May 89			6	6	
‡Interim pres	008		0	10Feb 89<	10Feb 89			0	0	
‡Product demo	009		0	05Jun 89<	05Jun 89			0	0	
‡Project report	010		9	16Mar 89	07Jun 89			54	12	
‡Project viva	011		0	19Jun 89<	19Jun 89			0	0	
‡Project mngmnt	012		33	09Nov 88	21Jun 89			14	0	

Resource Details
23May 89   4:21p

Rsrc Name:My Name   One Person Project Resource

Total Overscheduled: 273   Rate Mult:1.00
Calendar Variance: 0   No.Units: 1
Workday: Sun Mon Tue Wed Thu Fri Sat   Defaults   Hours: 40   Totals
Start: 9:00a 0   0   8   8   8   4   0   Standard Day: 8
                                                Allocation: 60xx   Hrs: 578

ID	Task	Dur	Hrs	Allc	Un	Ovr	Pr	Start	Finish
001	Choose project	2	12	75xx	1	0	50	05Oct 88	12Oct 88
002	Terms of ref	3	18	75xx	1	0	50	12Oct 88	26Oct 88
003	Initial plan	2	12	75xx	1	9	50	12Oct 88	19Oct 88
026	Fact finding	6	36	75xx	1	0	50	26Oct 88	17Nov 88
012	Project mngmnt	33	14	5xx	1	0	50	09Nov 88	21Jun 89
027	Modelling	7	42	75xx	1	1	50	17Nov 88	11Jan 89
028	Input design	4	24	75xx	1	19	50	11Jan 89	26Jan 89
029	Output design	4	24	75xx	1	24	50	11Jan 89	26Jan 89
030	File design	6	36	75xx	1	29	50	11Jan 89	08Feb 89
031	Process design	5	30	75xx	1	1	50	11Jan 89	01Feb 89
013	Build A	5	30	75xx	1	21	50	08Feb 89	01Mar 89
016	Build B	5	30	75xx	1	30	50	08Feb 89	01Mar 89
019	Build C	5	30	75xx	1	0	50	08Feb 89	01Mar 89
008	Interim pres	0	0	75xx	1	4	50	10Feb 89	10Feb 89
014	Test A	4	24	75xx	1	19	50	01Mar 89	16Mar 89
017	Test B	6	36	75xx	1	29	50	01Mar 89	10May 89
020	Test C	5	30	75xx	1	12	50	01Mar 89	12Apr 89
010	Project report	9	54	75xx	1	12	50	16Mar 89	07Jun 89
015	Link A	2	12	75xx	1	12	50	16Mar 89	10May 89
021	Link C	2	12	75xx	1	10	50	12Apr 89	10May 89
018	Link B	2	12	75xx	1	14	50	10May 89	17May 89
022	System test	3	18	75xx	1	12	50	17May 89	31May 89
023	User training	2	12	75xx	1	6	50	17May 89	24May 89
025	Installation	1	6	75xx	1	8	50	31May 89	31May 89
024	Data loading	4	24	75xx	1	0	50	31May 89	21Jun 89
009	Product demo	0	0	75xx	1	0	50	05Jun 89	05Jun 89
011	Project viva	0	0	75xx	1	0	50	19Jun 89	19Jun 89

```
Task Details                                      Project: MY-PROJ.PJ
23May 89   4:20p                                        Revision: 0

  ID: 025                                                          +
  Name:Installation

                              Start            Finish      Totals
  Duration: 1          Schd:31May 89        31May 89   Hrs:    6
                                            Priority:         Ovr: 6

  Resource Hrs Allc Un    Predecessors      Successors        Lag

  My Name   6 75%x  1 022 System test    FS 024 Data loading  FS  0h
                      023 User training  FS
```

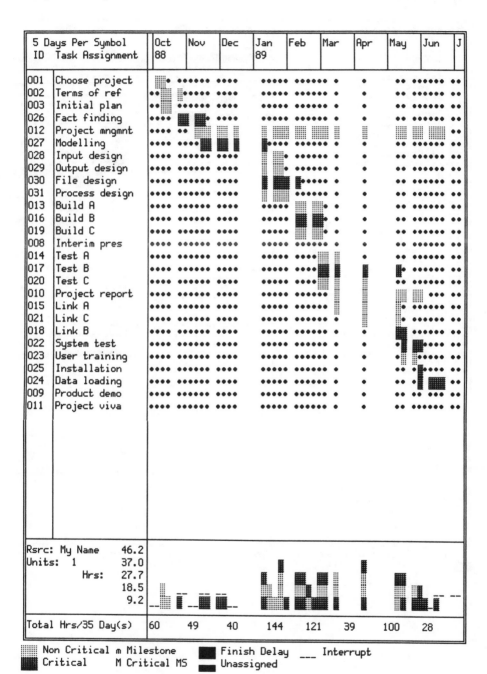

| 5 Days Per Symbol | Oct | Nov | Dec | Jan | Feb | Mar | Apr | May | Jun | J |
ID Task Assignment	88			89						
001 Choose project										
002 Terms of ref										
003 Initial plan										
026 Fact finding										
012 Project mngmnt										
027 Modelling										
028 Input design										
029 Output design										
030 File design										
031 Process design										
013 Build A										
016 Build B										
019 Build C										
008 Interim pres										
014 Test A										
017 Test B										
020 Test C										
010 Project report										
015 Link A										
021 Link C										
018 Link B										
022 System test										
023 User training										
025 Installation										
024 Data loading										
009 Product demo										
011 Project viva										

Rsrc: My Name   46.2
Units: 1   37.0
        Hrs: 27.7
                   18.5
                    9.2

| Total Hrs/35 Day(s) | 60 | 49 | 40 | 144 | 121 | 39 | 100 | 28 |

Non Critical m Milestone   Finish Delay   ___ Interrupt
Critical   M Critical MS Unassigned

127

5 Days Per Symbol	Oct	Nov	Dec	Jan	Feb	Mar	Apr	N
ID Heading/Task	88			89				

ID	Heading/Task
P1	MY-PROJ.PJ
001	±Choose project
002	±Terms of ref
003	±Initial plan
004	Spec of reqs
026	± Fact finding
027	± Modelling
005	Detailed design
028	± Input design
029	± Output design
030	± File design
031	± Process design
006	Program build
013	± Build A
014	± Test A
015	± Link A
016	± Build B
017	± Test B
018	± Link B
019	± Build C
020	± Test C
021	± Link C
007	Implementation
022	± System test
023	± User training
024	± Data loading
025	± Installation
008	±Interim pres
009	±Product demo
010	±Project report
011	±Project viva
012	±Project mngmnt

Non Critical   m Milestone   Finish Delay   ___ Interrupt
Critical   M Critical MS   Unassigned

Jul	Aug	Sep	Oct	Nov	Dec	Jan 90	Feb	Mar	Apr	May	Jun

Project: MY-PROJ.PJ

Calendar for: Project

Range: 11May 89 to 11May 89

1989	Sun	O Mon	8 Tue	8 Wed	8 Thu	8 Fri	8 Sat	O
Apr May	30 WKND	01 BANK HOL	02 EXAMS	03 EXAMS	04 EXAMS	05 EXAMS	06 WKND	
May	07 WKND	08	09	10	22 11	7 12	13 WKND	

ID	Task Assignment	Resource	Hrs	Allc	Un	Dur	Start	Finish	C
010	Project report	My Name	54	75%xx	1	9	16Mar 89	07Jun 89	
012	Project mngmnt	My Name	14	5%xx	1	33	09Nov 88	21Jun 89	
018	Link B	My Name	12	75%xx	1	2	10May 89	17May 89	

APPENDIX B

Project management and personal time management forms

1. Monitoring sheet

2. Periodic progress report

3. Daily time analysis chart

4. Key areas form

5. Work element list

6. Year plan

7. Weekly schedule

8. Daily plan

Project Monitoring Sheet

Name: _ _ _ _ _ _ _ _   Project: _ _ _ _ _ _ _ _   Version No: _ _ _ _ _ _ _ _   Date: _ _ _ _ _ _ _ _

Project Weeks

Ref No	Description	1	2	3	4	5	6	7	8	9	10	11	12	13	14	15	16	17	18	19	20	21	22	23	24	25	26	27	28	29	30	31	32	33	34	35

Check points
Time now
Days per week
Week commencing (Calender day)

△ Start / finish event   ▲ Rescheduled event   ▲ Completed event   o Checkpoint   ● Completed checkpoint   ↑ Time now

132

PERIODIC PROGRESS REPORT

Number: ....

Date: ....

Name: .... Project: ....

A. Current Situation

B. Contacts Made (with dates)

C. Problem Areas and Solutions

D. Key Work During Next Review Period

Date of Next Review ....

D. becomes the control yardstick for A. at the next review.
C. encourages solutions to be put forward even if it requires supervisor intervention.

time of day	no of mins	activity	key area	idea for improvement
Daily Time Analysis Chart		day of week:		date:
0800				
0900				
1000				
1100				
1200				
1300				
1400				
1500				
1600				
1700				
1800				
1900				
2000				
2100				
2200				

KEY AREAS	
1	
2	
3	
4	
5	
6	
7	
8	
9	
NOTES	

WORK ELEMENT LIST		KEY AREA	
NO	DETAILS	DUE DATE / /	DONE

MONTH	WK/C / /	WK NO			
SEP					
OCT					
NOV					
DEC					
JAN					
FEB					
MAR					
APR					
MAY					
JUN					
JUL					
AUG					

TIME	MON	TUE	WED	THU	FRI	SAT	SUN
0800							
0900							
1000							
1100							
1200							
1300							
1400							
1500							
1600							
1700							
1800							
1900							
2000							
2100							
2200							
NOTES							

DAY:	/ /

MAJOR WORK OF DAY

0800	**DAY'S WORK ELEMENT LIST**
0900	
1000	
1100	
1200	
1300	**NOTES**
1400	
1500	
1600	
1700	
1800	**DON`T FORGET**
1900	
2000	
2100	
2200	

BIBLIOGRAPHY

Anderson, J., Durston, B.H., and *Poole, M.*, Thesis and assignment writing, John Wiley and Sons (Australia 1970).

Austin, B., Making effective use of executive time, Management Update Limited (London 1986).

Barrass, R., Students must write, Methuen (London 1982).

Cooper, B.M., Writing technical reports, Penguin (London 1966).

Gower, E., Complete plain words, Penguin (London 1962).

Janner, G., Janner's complete speechmaker, Business Books Limited (London 1984).

Jones, E., Effective writing, Ward Lock (London 1974).

Lloyd, S.M., Roget's Thesaurus, Longman (London 1982).

Mitchell, J., How to write reports, Fontana (London 1974).

Morse, S.P., The practical approach to business presentations, Management Update Limited (London 1985).

Sillars, S., Success in communication, John Murray (Publishers) (London 1988).

Sykes, J.B., The concise Oxford dictionary, Oxford University Press (Oxford 1988).

Wainwright, G., Report writing, Management Update Limited (London 1984).

Waller, C., Using your overhead projector and other visual aids, Fordigraph (London 1983).

Weiner, E.S.C., The Oxford guide to the English language, Oxford University Press (Oxford 1987).

Yeates, D., Systems project management, Pitman Publishing (London 1986).

Simon Rogerson BSc MBIM MIDPM

As a graduate from the University of Dundee, Simon Rogerson started his career in Computing over 17 years ago as a scientific programmer. He quickly progressed into the systems analysis area working on commercial and scientific computer projects. In his later industrial career, he held the positions of Systems Development Manager and Computer Services Manager before taking up a lecturing post at Leicester Polytechnic. He currently holds the post of Principal Lecturer in the Department of Information Systems specialising in management related issues in Computing and Information Technology. He maintains his links with industry by undertaking consultancy assignments in the areas of business systems analysis and project management. As an active member of the Institute of Data Processing Management, he serves on the national education committee and is a member of Council.